VIOLENCE AGAINST GIRL CHILD IN SCHOOLS

About the Author

Prof. (Dr.) Lokanath Mishra, earned M.Sc. (Math), M.A (Eco) M.Ed. Ph.D. (Education), D.Litt. (Education) presently working as Professor and Head, Department of Education, Mizoram University (A Central University) Aizawl, Mizoram. Previously he was working as Director, Faculty Development Center, Mizoram University, Principal in the rank of professor in Vivek College of Education, Bijnor (UP). He had been trained on Leadership for Academicians Programme (LEAP) through University of Pennsylvania, USA under Pandit Madan Mohan Malvya National Mission on Teacher and Teaching (PMMMNMTT), Ministry of Education, Government of India. Prof. Mishra was the Senior fellow of ICSSR, New Delhi. As National Coordinator of National Resource Centre he has developed 40 modules (both Video and Text) on Educational Research for Annual Refresher Programme in Teaching (ARPIT) meant for Higher Education faculty using the MOOCs platform SWAYAM under Ministry of Education, Government of India. Prof. Mishra visited eight countries USA, Turkey, Fiji, Cyprus, Malaysia North Cyrus, Nepal and Indonesia as academic resource person and published 105 papers ,19 books and 32 chapters in an edited book. Prof. Mishra is the Editor in Chief of two International Journals and Editorial Board member of 15 journals of international repute.

VIOLENCE AGAINST GIRL CHILD IN SCHOOLS

Lokanath Mishra

CONCEPT PUBLISHING COMPANY PVT. LTD.
NEW DELHI - 110 059

ISBN: 978-93-5594-652-2

First Published 2024

Published and Printed by

Concept
Since 1974

Concept Publishing Company Pvt. Ltd.
A/15-16, Commercial Block, Mohan Garden
New Delhi-110059 (India)
T: +91-11-41101460
E: publishing@conceptpub.com, *W*: www.conceptpub.com

Cataloging in Publication--Courtesy: D.K. Agencies (P) Ltd. <docinfo@dkagencies.com>

Mishra, Lokanath (*College teacher*), **author.**
Violence against girl child in schools / Lokanath Mishra.
pages cm
Includes bibliographical references and index.
ISBN 9789355946522

1. Schoolgirls--Violence against--India--Mizoram. 2. Schoolgirls--Violence against--Prevention--Government policy--India--Mizoram. I. Title.

LCC HV6250.4.G57M57 2024 | DDC 362.880820954166 23

Preface

This work is based upon the project the Ministry of Women and Child Development, Government of India, conferred to me. This volume of 'Violence against Women' has been prepared to give students, parents, and teachers a voice and gather insight into their views on gender-based violence against girls in secondary schools in Mizoram.

This has been done through an exploratory-cum-descriptive research design. This book will have qualitative and quantitative methodologies (mixed-mode method) to study the nature, nuances, and best practices adopted by the school to mitigate violence against girls in secondary schools. It discusses the causes, types and strategies to deal with violence against girls in secondary schools. In chapter two, it provides comprehensive reviews of literature, including different types of violence. It thoroughly discusses the theories of crime against women and girls. Interestingly, the third chapter includes a detailed account of the research methodology, including the tools used. The fourth chapter deals with data analyses and a summary of the interpretations. Most significantly, the fifth chapter attempts to provide a deep evaluation of government policies and strategies pertaining to violence against girls and women.

While practising and researching in teacher education (pre-service teacher training programme to prepare secondary school teachers), I realized the need and scope of revisiting and reconstructing concepts, theories and framework of violence against girls. This book is inspired by the perceived need to bring secondary school teachers into the arena of violence-free education, but not without a sound understanding of the ground reality of violence against girls. I built an effective and comprehensive framework to understand the issue and suggest remedies to hinder violence against girls.

This book shall act beneficial in developing effective and comprehensive intervention programs by understanding the perceptions of violence and obtaining a perception of how to develop school-based violence prevention programmes. I took up this book-writing project to create a sourcebook on violence against women and girls. The consolidated study shall act as a stepping stone to suggest the Government, teachers, and parents deal with violence in schools, and is bound to have over-arching implications on all concerned institutions and stakeholders.

Lokanath Mishra

Acknowledgements

First and foremost, I am highly thankful to the Ministry of Women and Child Development, Government of India for providing financial support for conducting this need-based and time honored project. The project team acknowledges the help of all the experts who have extended their kind help by giving valuable suggestions in the preparation of the tools used for the present study.

We were extended all encouragements and support whenever and wherever needed. My sincere thanks in same quanta are due to Prof. Rabindra Kumar Mohanty, Head, Department of Sociology, Mizoram University for his encouragement throughout the journey. I feel indebted to all Professors, external as well as internal, teachers from schools, Government officials and NGO personnel who contributed a lot in the workshops organized at various stages of accomplishment of this project.

The government officials of Mizoram State Child Protection Society, Mizoram State Commission for Women, Directorate of Social Welfare, District Child Protection Unit, and the NGO Centre for Peace and Development deserve appreciation for providing the required information available with them in connection with the project.

I also express my gratitude to all the teachers and students of secondary schools of Mizoram for their co-operation without which it would not have been possible to complete the task.

Last but not the least, I acknowledge the work and sincerity of the three project fellows namely—Samuel L. Chuaungo, F. Zosangliani, and Laltlanzauvi Kawlni.

Lokanath Mishra

Contents

List of Tables and Figures

Tables

Figures

Abbreviations

ACA	:	Adoption Coordinating Agency
ACHR	:	Asian Centre for Human Rights
AG	:	Adolescent Girls
AIDS	:	Acquired Immune Deficiency Syndrome
AMKA	:	All Mizoram Karate Association
BEO	:	Block Education Officer
CCL	:	Children in Conflict with Law
CEDAW	:	Convention on the Elimination of All Forms of Discrimination against Women
CNCP	:	Children in Need of Care and Protection
CPD	:	Centre for Peace and Development
CRC	:	Convention on the Rights of the Child
CSA	:	Childhood Sexual Abuse
DCPU	:	District Child Protection Units
DEO	:	District Education Officer
DoNER	:	Development of North Eastern Region
FGD	:	Focus Group Discussion
GBV	:	Gender-Based Violence
GER	:	Gross Enrolment Ratio
GOI	:	Government of India
HIV	:	Human Immune Virus
ICDS	:	Integrated Child Development Services
ICPS	:	The Integrated Child Protection Scheme
ICSSR	:	Indian Council of Social Science Research
ICT	:	Information & Communication Technology
IPV	:	Intimate Partner Violence

JJBs	:	Juvenile Justice Boards
KSY	:	Kishori Shakti Yojana
MATA	:	Mizoram Amateur Taekwondo Association
MDG	:	Millennium Development Goals
MSCPS	:	Mizoram State Child Protection Society
NEC	:	North Eastern Council
NEDFi	:	North Eastern Development Finance Corporation Ltd
NGOs	:	Non-Governmental Organizations
NPE	:	National Policy on Education
PAB	:	Project Appraisal Board
PTA	:	Parents Teachers Association
SAA	:	Specialized Adoption Agencies
SAARC	:	South Asian Association for Regional Cooperation
SARA	:	State Adoption Resource Agency
SES	:	Socio Economic Status
SJPU	:	Special Juvenile Police Units
SLT	:	Social Learning Theory
TTI	:	Teachers Training Institute
UK	:	United Kingdom
UNCHR	:	United Nations Commissioner for Human Rights
UNCRC	:	United Nations Convention on the Rights of the Child
UNDP	:	United Nations Development Programme
UNESCO	:	United Nations Education, Scientific and Cultural Organization
UNICEF	:	United Nations International Children's Emergency Fund
UNICEF	:	United Nations Children's Fund
UNIFEM	:	United Nations Development Fund for Women
USAID	:	United States Agency for International Development
VAW	:	Violence against Women
WHO	:	World Health Organization
YMA	:	Young Man's Association

1
Introduction

1.0 The Problem Studied

Debates and discourses on girl child in particular relating to abuse, discrimination and gender-based violence are on the increase during last three and half decades. Violence against women and girls is one of the most systematic and widespread human rights violations. It is rooted in gendered social structures rather than individual and random acts; it cuts across age, socio-economic, educational and geographic boundaries; affects all societies; and is a major obstacle to ending gender inequality and discrimination globally (UN General Assembly, 2006).

Violence is defined by the World Health Organization as 'the intentional use of physical force or power, threatened or actual, against oneself, another person, or against a group or community, which either results in or has a high likelihood of resulting in injury, death, psychological harm, mal development, or deprivation'. This definition involves intentionally with the committing of the act itself, irrespective of the outcome it produces. Violence in many forms is preventable. There is a strong relationship between levels of violence and modifiable factors such as concentrated poverty, income and gender inequality, the harmful use of alcohol, and the absence of safe, stable, and nurturing relationships between children and parents. Strategies addressing the underlying causes of violence can be effective in preventing violence.

A child is a human species below eighteen years of age who is in need of care of and protection because of tender age and inexperienced personality, irrespective whether a boy or a girl (Mohanty 2016:140). *Webster's dictionary* defines a girl as any female human from birth through childhood and adolescence to attainment of adulthood when she becomes a woman. The term may also be used to mean a woman in becoming.

The United Nations defines violence against women as "any act of gender-based violence that results in, or is likely to result in, physical, sexual or psychological harm or suffering to women, including threats of such acts, coercion or arbitrary deprivation of liberty, whether occurring in public or in private life" (General Assembly Resolution 48/104 Declaration on the Elimination of Violence Against Women, 1993). The United Nations defines violence against women as:

> "*Any act of gender-based violence that results in, or is likely to result in, physical, sexual or psychological harm or suffering to women, including threats of such acts, coercion or arbitrary deprivation of liberty, whether occurring in public or private life. Accordingly, violence against women encompasses but is not limited to the following: (a) Physical, sexual and psychological violence occurring in the family, including battering, sexual abuse of female children in the household, dowry-related violence, marital rape, female genital mutilation and other traditional practices harmful to women, non-spousal violence and violence related to exploitation; (b) Physical, sexual and psychological violence occurring within the general community, including rape, sexual abuse, sexual harassment and intimidation at work, in educational institutions and elsewhere, trafficking in women and forced prostitution; (c) Physical, sexual and psychological violence perpetrated or condoned by the State, wherever it occurs*" (General Assembly Resolution 48/104 Declaration on the Elimination of Violence against Women, 1993).

Given the absence of a specific definition for minors, the above definition is taken to refer to women of all ages, including girls. Violence against women and girls is a major health and human rights issue. At least one in five of the world's female population has been physically or sexually abused by a man or men at some time in their life. Many including pregnant women and young girls are subject to severe, sustained or repeated attacks. It has been estimated that violence against women worldwide is as serious a cause of death and incapacity among women of reproductive age as cancer, and a greater cause of ill-health as traffic accidents and malaria combined. The abuse of women is effectively condoned in almost every society of the world. Prosecution and conviction of men who beat or rape women or girls is rare when compared to number of assaults. Violence, therefore, operates as a means to maintain and reinforce women's subordination.

Beginning before birth, in some countries, with sex-selective abortions, or at birth when female babies may be killed by parents who are desperate for a son, it continues to affect women throughout their lives. Each year, millions of girls undergo female genital mutilation. Female children are more likely than their brothers to be raped or sexually assaulted by family members, by those in positions of trust or power, or by strangers. In some countries, when an unmarried woman or adolescent is raped, she may be forced to marry her attacker, or she may be imprisoned for committing criminal act. Those women who become pregnant before marriage may be beaten or murdered by family members, even if the pregnancy is the result of a rape.

Violence in schools affects both boys and girls. Sexual and gender-based violence directed to girls is a particular concern. A related concern is the lack in all regions of reliable and comparable data of violence against girls in or related to schools and education. Studies from certain European countries indicate that boys are generally subject to violence more often than girls, but that girls to a larger extent than boys are victims of certain severe forms of violence, including sexual violence. Between 15-20 per cent of girls are estimated to have experienced such violence before the age of 16.

The types of violence range from assault and harassment on the way to and from school to bullying, sexual harassment and mental and physical abuse in education faculties, including as means of corporal punishment. Violence is not limited to primary and secondary schools but is also reported from tertiary education, often in the form of sexual coercion and harassment. Demand for sexual favours by teachers and classmates in return for covering school transport, education fees or other school-related costs are regularly reported from countries where education is not free in accordance with international human rights law. Even without such enticements girls and young women may feel coerced and fear the consequences of refusing advances.

The direct impacts on girls' education, and indirect impact on their enjoyment of other human rights, have been identified in several national contexts. The threat or risk of violence may discourage parents from sending their daughters to school. This is particularly true for conflict-situations and areas where the journey to education-facilities is long, and there is a risk for assault and abductions on the way to school. Drop-out levels and learning difficulties are significantly higher among victim of violence, thus a serious obstacle to gender equality and empowerment of future generations of women.

Violence in schools cannot be divorced from violence in the home, the community and the workplace. This violence originates in the imbalance of power between males and females, in the gendered hierarchy and separation of tasks and in socially accepted views of what constitutes masculine and feminine behaviour. The school, alongside the home, is a prime site for the construction of gender identity and gender relations built on socially sanctioned inequalities. The structures and practices that fill the school day with explicit and implicit rules, norms and symbols serve to guide and regulate behaviour; in so doing, they reinforce the unequal gender relations already reproduced in the home and perpetuate notions of male superiority and dominance Examples include teacher tolerance of male students' domination of classroom space at the expense of girls' participation in lessons; the celebration of masculine competitiveness; the allocation of more public and higher status tasks and responsibilities to male students and teachers, and private domestic-related ones to female students and teachers; the acceptance of bullying and verbal abuse as a natural part of growing up; and teachers' unofficial use of free student labour, especially that of girls. These taken-for-granted, routine practices of schooling all too often teach children that masculinity is associated with aggression, while femininity requires obedience, acquiescence and making oneself attractive to boys. In this way, male violence becomes accepted in adolescent relationships and thus perpetuated into adulthood. This dominant version of gender relations promoted by the school is almost exclusively framed in terms of a compulsory heterosexuality. Males seeking to strengthen their status among their peers may interpret this as the need to show dominance over females. This encourages gratuitous acts of sexual harassment, such as boys cornering and groping girls or shouting demeaning obscenities, and male teachers making sexist or derogatory comments to female students or teachers, or making physical contact with girls during lessons. Despite the importance attached to discipline by school authorities in the developing world, acts of gender violence often go unreported and unpunished. Students may not report incidents out of fear of victimization, punishment or ridicule, or because violence is seen as an inevitable and accepted part of school life. Even if they do, teachers often consider such incidents as not worthy of reprimand. In many parts of the world, there are poor levels of accountability in the educational system and a lack of good management and professional commitment. Evidence from Sub-Saharan Africa suggests that teachers who exploit the advantage of their sex and their authority by having sexual relations with students are rarely expelled from the teaching profession, even in cases of pregnancy; at most, an offending teacher will be transferred to another school. To complicate matters, not all parents, teachers and girls disapprove of teachers or older men having sexual liaisons with schoolgirls, whether for economic or cultural reasons.

Societies, rich and poor alike, are increasingly articulating commitments that guarantee girls safe and equal access to entitlements, services, social participation, and economic opportunities. Yet threats of violence in many forms—culturally affirmed (child marriage, female genital mutilation), intimate (carried out by family members and partners), casual (carried out by strangers), and planned (trafficking)—intervene to prevent girls from claiming their rights. Many countries are signatories to the Convention on the Elimination of All Forms of Discrimination against Women (CEDAW) and the Convention on the Rights of the Child (CRC), and stipulate equality between males and females in their constitutions. Theoretically, safe access to resources and facilities is equally afforded to girls and boys; however a far higher proportion of boys and a smaller subset of usually more privileged girls may actually claim their rights and opportunities. Girls' lives are often conditioned around the possibility of violence. And acts of violence exert additional power over girls because the stigma of violence often attaches more to a girl than to her perpetrator. The experience of violence is devastating at the individual emotional and physical level. Its power to interrupt or fully disable girls' access to entitlements, social participation, and—crucially—safe and decent livelihoods is an equally compelling reason. Violence is so pervasive in many societies that it has the feeling of being an active "plan" or even an opposing sector undermining the investments made by other sectors in girls' well-being. Part of the "plan" to deny the rights of girls, even when society has made progress, are to condition them to avoid opportunity in order to manage risk. As girls internalize their responsibility for managing this risk, they begin to precensor their potential to stop it. The proportion of affected girls who report sexual violence is very low; in some settings, only about half of girls who experience sexual violence tell someone about the abuse. The process through which girls must report violence can traumatize them. In some settings, access to services is a barrier in and of itself, as many communities have few or no services for survivors of violence. Authorities and service providers' rarely have training on how to treat cases of violence and even fewer people are trained on how to treat girl survivors of violence.

1.1 Theoretical Context

Theories of crime against women and girls are explained in terms of four theories: (1) Gender Theory, (2) Theories of Vulnerabilities, (3) Theories of Victimization, and (4) Typology of Violence.

Gender Theory: The women-specific approach is complex. It can sometimes be progressive, liberal or conservative depending on how it is used, who uses it and for what purposes. Thus, feminism as a whole brought a greater structural distance between men and women. Amidst all these controversies emerged the concept of gender relations. Can men without women or women without men be thought of? Feminists and women activists opposed the use of the word gender because it diverts from the specific problem of women.

Social scientists and development experts still use two separate terms to designate biologically determined differences between men and women, which are called "sex differences", and those constructed socially, which are called "gender differences". Both define the differences between men and women, but they have very different connotations. Gender as a concept went much beyond biological category of sex or masculinity or feminist.

The gendered perspective does not look at women and men alone, but at the relationship between them, how societies are structured along gender lines and the impact of these relations in the whole society. This approach explores the subordination of women to men and how this relationship impacts on all aspects of life and society. That relationship is not experienced in the same way everywhere. The context in which gendered relationships emerge and the constantly shifting economic, political and social ground is always recognized. A gendered perspective is concerned with ensuring a gender analysis with regard to policies, programmes, planning strategy and evaluation. In other words, it looks at fundamentally transforming unequal power relations and changing society. The gender perspective looks at the impact of gender on people's opportunities, social roles and interactions. Successful implementation of the policy, programme and project goals of international and national organizations is directly affected by the impact of gender and, in turn, influences the process of social development. Gender is an integral component of every aspect of the economic, social, daily and private lives of individuals and societies, and of the different roles ascribed by society to men and women. This is what is now popularly known as 'gender main streaming'.

A useful way to view gender violence is by identifying the concept of hierarchical gender relations, where the violence towards women occurs. Essentially, violence happens in three contexts (Schuler, 1992)—the family, the community and the state and at each point key social institutions fulfil critical and interactive functions in defining legitimating and maintaining the violence. (1) The family socialises its members to accept hierarchical relations expressed in unequal division of labour between the sexes and power over the allocation of resources. (2) The community (i.e., social, economic, religious, and cultural institutions) provides the mechanisms for perpetuating male control over women's sexuality, mobility and labour. (3) The state legitimises the proprietary rights of men over women, providing a legal basis to the family and the community to perpetuate these relations. The state does this through the enactment of discriminatory application of the law.

Gender violence is defined as "any act involving use of force or coercion with intent of perpetuating promoting hierarchical gender relations" (Schuler, 1992). Thus, the use of the term gender-based violence (GBV)—provides a new context in which to examine and understand the long-standing phenomenon of violence against women shifts the focus from women as victims to gender and the unequal power relationships between women and men created and maintained by gender stereotypes as the basic underlying cause of violence against women (VAW). GBV is a cause and consequence of inequality between sexes, gender stereotypes, discrimination and roles. Women are more vulnerable.

Theories of Vulnerabilities: The hardest challenge to take in life is being a girl child. Discrimination, differences, dominance, disadvantage, drudgery and discrepancy are six most Vitamin D deficiencies under social pathology that hamper the journey of every female from womb to tomb. Starting from her presence into her mother's womb to infancy, childhood and finally to adulthood and age, she is under the stranglehold of notorious traditions and stereotypical myths. Social disadvantage outweighs natural biological advantage of being a girl (Mohanty 2016: 156). There are several illustrations of girls being neglected, denied equity in food, education, health care, being subject to serious physical and sexual abuse (Government of India, 2007), and marginalized in opportunities for developing and expressing their independent identity. They are subjected to what can be considered the rhetoric of a society in which they are considered "*paraayadhan*" (which literally translates to property of another/ other). There is an over-emphasis on the female's domestic role—, i.e. daughter, daughter-in-law, wife, mother, mother-in-law, grandmother and other domesticated social roles. These roles become enlarged in her psychic conditioning at home, at school and in the community, throughout the process of her growing up— both directly, as well as indirectly.

Girls are the most vulnerable in the society. It should be noted that there is somewhat of a causal connection between "means of protection" and "protection risks" in that poor access to birth, education and property rights (all regarded as means of protection) have the potential to increase exposure to risks such as child labour, trafficking, commercial sexual exploitation and underage marriage. Such risks relate directly to the exploitation of girls, and have many flow-on effects in terms of impeding the ability of girls to realize their full potential and participate effectively in society. There is also often a causal link between risk factors and means of protection, as where underage marriage or trafficking can lead to diminished possibilities for access to education.

Nobel Laureate Amartya Sen (2011) argued that the overall statistics on the condition of women with special reference to the young has been extremely pernicious. Shantha Sinha (2008) has detailed out the girl specific vulnerabilities in her keynote address at the Symposium on "Girl Child" in Panjab University, Chandigarh during their Diamond Jubilee celebrations. Denying girls opportunities—whether purposefully through discriminatory laws or tacitly through policies that fail to deter abuse, ensure control over reproduction, or prevent life-threatening disease—substantially undermines the creation of human capital endowments in society. The fact, that improvements in a woman's economic position do have a positive spill-over effect on the social welfare of her children.

Theories of Victimization: A victim is a person subjected to cruelty, oppression, or other harsh or unfair treatment, or suffering death, injury, ruin, harm or loss physical, emotional or pecuniary, as a result of an event, circumstance or oppressive or adverse action of the perpetrator(s) (Mohanty, 2016). Hierarchy, inequality, and violence have always been part of human social structures and cultures. There were always rulers and ruled, leaders and followers, the fortunate and the needy, the powerful and the weak. Various cultures have treated disparities in status, power, fortune, and ability in different ways. Girl children, in particular, are worst victimized in many societies (Kury, Helmut *et al.,* 2016).

Although children do suffer from all the crimes that adults do, many violent and deviant behaviour by human actors that harm children are ambiguous in their status as crimes. The physical abuse of children, although technically criminal, is not frequently prosecuted and generally is handled by a different set of social control agencies from the police and criminal courts. Peer assaults, unless very serious or occurring among older children, are generally ignored by the official criminal justice system.

Finkelhor (2007) has proposed that the victimization of children be defined as including three categories: (1) conventional crimes in which children are victims (rape, robbery, assault), which I will call "crimes"; (2) acts that violate child welfare statutes, including some of the most serious and dangerous acts committed against children, such as abuse and neglect, but also some less frequently discussed topics such as the exploitation of child labour, which is termed "child maltreatment"; and (3) acts that would clearly he crimes if committed by adults against adults, but by convention, are not generally of concern in the criminal justice system when they occur among or against children. These would include sibling violence and assaults between preadolescent peers, and those that might be termed "non-criminal juvenile crime equivalents," which is called "non-crimes" (*Ibid.*: 10-11).

1.2 Typology of Violence

The complexity, pervasiveness and variety of violent acts, prompt feelings of powerlessness and apathy. An analytical framework or typology is needed to separate the threads of this intricate tapestry so that the nature of the problem—and the action required dealing with it—becoming clearer. Up to now, work to counter violence has been fragmented into specialized areas of research and action. To overcome this shortcoming, the analytical framework should emphasize the common features and linkages between different types of violence, leading to a holistic approach to prevention. Few such typologies exist, and none is comprehensive or universally accepted.

The typology also captures the nature of violent acts, which can be physical, sexual or psychological or involve deprivation or neglect. The typology also considers the relevance of the setting, the relationship between the perpetrator and victim, and—in the case of collective violence—the possible motives for the violence. Margaret Schuler (1992) has divided gender violence into four major categories:

1. Overt physical abuse (battering sexual assault, at home and in the work place),
2. Psychological abuse (confinement, forced marriage),
3. Deprivation of resources for physical and psychological wellbeing (health/nutrition, education, means of livelihood), and
4. Commodification of women (trafficking, prostitution).

Before one tackles the issue of violence on girls in secondary schools in Mizoram, one must first have a grasp on the general concept of violence and its varying types and degrees; and realise that the meaning of violence changes with time and place. Various writers have shown further light on the topic, but as the nature of academic studies goes, these writers cannot help but limit the scope of their studies to certain ethnographic sites and based within a predetermined time-frame. For the purposes of this project, therefore, we have here attempted a categorisation of the various types of violence that exists in academic studies before we tackle the relevance of these categorisations to the scenario in Mizoram.

Physical violence

Physical violence occurs when someone uses a part of their body or an object to control a person's actions. Physical violence includes, but is not limited to:

- A general usage of any form of physical force which results in pain, discomfort or injury of another person.
- This general usage of physical force can be further divided into the actual usage of a part or parts of one's body to inflict damage upon another person and includes hitting, pinching, hair-pulling, arm-twisting, strangling, burning, stabbing, punching, pushing, slapping, beating, shoving, kicking, choking, biting, force-feeding, or any other rough treatment.
- Physical force can take form in extensions of one's part or parts of the body by the usage of objects. Usually this is what we know as assault with a weapon or other object.
- Physical violence also includes acts where actual physical pain is not enforced. However, the possibility of receiving physical pain

imbues in the mind of the victim similar harm as receiving the actual physical pain itself. Therefore physical violence includes even threats—with one's body parts, weapons or objects.

- Besides the above mentioned acts where the victim experiences the brunt of physical violence by receiving either physical pain or the threat of physical pain, he or she may also face similar trauma in the form of being forced to experience uncomfortable physical environments. This includes deliberate exposure to severe weather or inappropriate room temperatures.
- Under this category, there is a sub-category of "restraints abuse"where a victim is harmed through the act of putting him or her under elongated periods of time under restraints. These include:

  - Forcible confinement in a limited physical space or area notably, for victims of kidnapping this is the first line of physical abuse that they have to face during their captivity.
  - Excessive, unwarranted or unnecessary use of physical restraints, this kind of restraint is closer to a victim's body and constraints him or her over and above confinement to a limited space or area. For example, if a victim has not only been confined to a room but also if he or she has been:
  - Tied to a bed or chair.
  - Forced to remain in bed.

Also called "chemical restraint", this type of violence includes usage of drugs or other chemicals. Such unwarranted use of medication is enforced to control victims either against their will or without their knowledge, and since it affects their body in negative ways, is considered physical violence as well.

Last but not the least, despite the finality of the result, murder by any means given above or otherwise, is considered to be a form of physical violence.

Sexual Violence

Sexual violence occurs when a person is forced to unwillingly take part in sexual activities or to be the recipient of sexual activities.

Sexual violence includes, but is not limited to:

- *Touching in a sexual manner without consent.* This type of violence includes kissing, grabbing and fondling among others.
- *Forced sexual intercourse.* Besides rape which is its most severe form, this type of abuse includes sexual intercourse where the victim is too scared or too unaware to understand the act as a form of abuse. Moreover, especially in the case of female victims, they may have been socially programmed to believe that the abuse is the way the patriarchal world works, and that it is their duty and role to accept the abuse as given.
- *Forcing a person to perform sexual acts that may be degrading or painful.* Sometimes even in a consensual relationship, a victim may be demanded to give in to certain sexual acts that are not only physically painful but also psychologically, mentally and spiritually degrading to the self. This kind of abuse is a major cause of low self-esteem especially among women.
- *Beating sexual parts of the body.* This kind of violence is similar to physical violence, with the only difference that the act has a specific goal of targeting sexual parts of the victim's body. Due to its effect on the victim's body and mind akin to acts of sexual violence, it can be categorized as such.
- *Using a weapon to force compliance.* This type of violence is similar to the above as physical violence is involved. Moreover, such violence is conducted to get a victim to comply with sexual demands.
- *Forced prostitution.* Even if one does not use violence for one's own sexual gratification, it can be used to satisfy others. This is true in the case of forced prostitution where the victim, due to pressure from various types of violence, is made to give in to a trade where she exchanges sexual favours in return for monetary benefits for someone else, i.e. the pimp.
- *Forcing a person to view pornographic material or forcing participation in pornographic filming.* Similar to prostitution, the world of pornography too is a dark one. Similar to the example given above, here too there is no self-gratification motive from the side of the oppressor. But due to its implications, getting

an unwilling victim to get involved with watching or enacting pornographic situations is considered sexual violence.

- *Humiliating, criticizing or trying to control a person's sexuality.* There are ways to enforce sexual violence even if it does not entail actual physical sexual acts or threats to make a victim give in to unwanted sexual demands. This would the case where a person is made uncomfortable regarding his or her sexuality or body. Humiliation, criticism and control of one's sexuality in the hands of another are just a few examples.
- *Making unwelcome sexual comments or jokes; leering behaviour.* This type of violence has become more visible in workplaces in recent times as awareness has grown. In fact, human resources departments of organizations and institutions deal with it very harshly now-a-days. But such kind of violence is not always reported for fear of work-related repercussions. Moreover, there are times when such atrocities are committed by those who are unaware of its effects on the victims. Realizing that such acts are inappropriate is the first step to counter this common form of sexual violence, followed by appropriate measures taken by those in authority to curb it completely in their jurisdictions.
- *Exhibitionism.* This form of sexual violence is a deviance that has been associated with mental imbalance in the perpetrator. However, this is no excuse for the infringement of not only personal space but also unwanted exposure to sexual parts of another person.
- *Denial of a person's sexuality or privacy.* Similar to the above, this type of violence is the other end of the spectrum where instead of being forced to watch others' sexual parts of the body, the victims are watched in secret instead. This kind of activity can further lead to the above mentioned sexual violence in pornography, where the element of secrecy is removed and the content is made public knowledge. Even though laws across the world are not yet fully conducive to the best interests of the victims, it is at least a start.
- *Withholding sexual affection.* This particular type of violence is a little controversial simply because of the lack of sexual activity. However, keeping in mind domestic issues arising out of the

inactivity of one of the two partners, it is very feasible for such inactivity to be categorized as a sexual violence.

Emotional Violence

Emotional violence occurs when someone says or does something to make a person feel stupid or worthless. Emotional violence includes, but is not limited to:

- *Name calling.* When one resorts to name calling, he or she is inflicting damage based on the victim's already existing insecurities. This causes not only emotional trauma in the moment but also long lasting effects in the victim's mind. Moreover, the victim tends to worsen his or her emotional insecurities if it is fuelled by constant name calling.
- *Blaming all relationship problems on the person.* A relationship involves more than a single individual, and in that effect, all burdens should either be shared or compartmentalized. When blame goes on a single partner as the source of all problems, that person tends to harbour guilt and insecurity resulting in low self-esteem and maldevelopment.
- *Not allowing the person to have contact with family and friends.* Man is a social animal and needs the intimacy of physical proximity as well as social acceptance. Particularly at younger ages, the source of these intimate relationships stems from family and friends. Even at a later stage, particularly in the case of women in a patriarchal setup, there is a tendency of curbing the woman's range of social interactions from both friends as well as natal homes. This has come to be widely known as a form of emotional violence as it hampers the very basics of social nourishment.
- *Destroying possessions.* Very often, the value of a physical object may extend beyond its monetary equivalence. For many, the length of time of possession of an object proportionately relates to the amount of sentimental attachment to the said object. When such a possession gets destroyed, most often despite the willingness of the owner, it results in a sense of trauma resulting from a sense of loss and the inability to fill up the

emotional void. In many cases, the repercussions of this trauma can arise after a long period of time in unhealthy manners and in an exponential degree. Unfortunately, such repercussions are accredited to a natural mental instability of the victim, or his or her "over reaction" to loss of a physical object; and the emotional aspects of the loss are seldom recognized.

- *Humiliating or making fun of the person.* A person does not belong to a single social group or setting alone. Depending on the different allegiances, a person's standing in society can be judged negatively based on gender, class, race, religion, caste etc. This can translate then to humiliation in the hands of others who do not share the same social circles. This not only discourages individual growth of the victim but also unfortunately sows seeds of further violence in his or her mind as a type of revenge mentality.
- *Intimidating the person, causing fear to gain control.* His is a more direct approach to the above mentioned violence. Here, rather than mockery and humiliation, the victim is put in immediate danger or threat of real danger. This may be either to simply gratify the violator or to gain control over the behaviour and free thought of the victim to bend according to the will of others. In both cases, it leaves no room for improvement at an emotional level in the victim; and while this harms the individual, it also harms the chances of harmony in a plural society as there will exist an outside ruling force.
- *Threatening to hurt one if the victim does not cooperate.* This is colloquially also known as emotional blackmail. This is a particularly disheartening type of violence as it exists only between parties that have a certain level of emotional attachment to one another. This heavily lowers the level of trust between the parties, especially if the actions are regularly enforced. Moreover, this hampers the ability of free and critical thought, and also leaves the victim in a state of perpetual guilt and caution in every action they undertake.
- *Threatening to abandon the person.* This is a more severe form of the above example and here the victim is usually a dependent of the one who is giving the threat. This dependence may be

both financial and emotional. Particularly in India, where the familial ties are stronger and last longer than it is in western societies, this threat is something that the victim cannot take chances with. Abandonment from someone that the victim is dependent on will result in an existential crisis where survival itself becomes a source of worry. Awareness has to be spread, particularly among patriarchs of Indian families, that this is an abuse of power that would only lead to emotional distress of their dependents.

Psychological Violence

Psychological violence occurs when someone uses threats and causes fear in a person to gain control. Psychological violence includes, but is not limited to:

- *Threatening to harm the person or her or his family if he or she leaves.* This kind of psychological violence occurs profusely in patriarchal setups where, on one hand, the woman or the wife becomes an important contributor to the familial life and household, but on the other, still holds a lower position in the stratification. Therefore, threats are often made to wives if they ever decide to leave the husband; and it becomes an easy solution for the patriarch to get his way where the woman not only gets confined to her new home, but also never rise from her social position in the household.
- *Threatening to harm one.* This is similar to the emotional violence mentioned earlier and moreover, similar to the example given above, there is a relationship of dependency of one partner on others.
- *Threats of abandonment.* Similarly, instead of threatening to harm one, there can be threats where even though no physical harm is involved; an equal amount of trauma can be inflicted upon the victim by the possibility of being abandoned by others. Here, it is interesting to note that such trauma can be a result of both physical and emotional dependency.
- *Stalking/criminal harassment.* The problem with stalking is that once a victim gets to know that he or she is being stalked, every

moment of her day is filled with fear. A step further is when the stalker opens up to the victim and confronts him or her that they are actively being stalked. This then becomes a very real and very dangerous situation for the victim where, besides the obvious awareness of the situation, the fear of the unknown or the fear of possible complications in the future starts to result in personal maldevelopment.

- *Socially isolating the person.* Similar to the emotional violence discussed earlier, lack of social relationships leads a victim to not only become psychologically isolated but also to become over-cautious in daily activities due to the absence of cushioning elements in everyday life.
- *Not allowing access to a telephone.* In today's day and age, phones have become a necessary part of modern life and influences not only social interactions but also work and finance related issues. Not only does banning access to telephones severely narrow down the size of the victim's social circle, but also rigorously dampen compatibility with modern life.
- *Not allowing a competent person to make decisions.* Particularly in households with an extremely strong patriarch, individuals rarely get to experience the gratification of feeling important as an adult contributing member of society because most of the important life decisions are taken by someone other than themselves. Such can also be applicable to the workplace or the relationship between a husband and wife, or parents and adult children. There then develops a psychological barricade that leads to dampening of leadership qualities, evaluation of one's self-worth, and even primary social acceptance.
- *Inappropriately controlling the person's activities.* A step further from the situation mentioned above, is the taking away of the ability of a person to engage in independent thought regarding even the minor aspects of everyday life. There thus starts a psychological dependence on the need for compatibility with the wishes of others, which may very well become an inconvenience in development of self-esteem and individual independence.

- *Treating a person like a child or a servant.* Particularly in developing economies like that in India, the value of manual labour still remains a financially unsound source of income. Moreover, the social position of manual labourers like servants, especially in the household, is a lowly one. Their contribution to society is considered similar to the efforts of a child in terms of adult decisions, and therefore, do not command respect. Therefore, being treated like a child or a servant becomes a huge blow to one's self-esteem, which if untreated or left to continue for prolonged periods of time, can lead to a psychological blockade.
- *Withholding companionship or affection.* Since every single individual is effectively a part of society, it becomes not only a natural process but a responsibility as well to offer and accept companionship and affection in social settings. Moreover, it is a responsibility to not bar others from engaging in such activities as well. The psychological effects on the victim in such a constrained situation are enough for the barring to be considered as violence.

Spiritual (or Religious) Violence

Spiritual (or religious) violence occurs when someone uses a person's spiritual beliefs to manipulate, dominate or control the person. Spiritual violence includes, but is not limited to:

- Not allowing the person to follow his or her preferred spiritual or religious tradition. Most countries of the world have an official stand of tolerance to various religions. Moreover, in India, the Constitution fundamentally gives its citizens the right to preach and practice any religion. These rules have come into being keeping in mind the importance of religion in an individual's all round nourishment. Prohibiting an individual from his or her spiritual goals is, therefore, a type of violence with very real implications.
- Forcing a spiritual or religious path or practice on another person. A step further from the above mentioned example is of forcing an individual to not only give up his or her spiritual

preference, but also to start following a completely different spiritual path or religion. Besides the negative effects on the individual, such violence can also be the cause of an unforgiving social setup where plurality is highly subdued and thus suppress free critical thought.

- Belittling or making fun of a person's spiritual or religious tradition, beliefs or practices. Even if an individual is not made to give up his or her own spirituality, or to follow a different religion, a same amount of damage can be inflicted upon them if they are made to feel that their own personal beliefs are inappropriate or not good enough. This then starts to mess with the victim's mind that perhaps they should give up on their individual choices simply due to peer pressure and their need to fit in a social setting.
- Using one's spiritual or religious position, rituals or practices to manipulate, dominate or control a person. This type of violence goes hand in hand with ideas of dominant discourse. In this kind of setting, there exists an idea that those few who have significant power over the majority due to their social, political, and economic prowess have the ability to establish "what should be". One of the elements affected in this philosophy of "what should be" is the idea of superiority of one religion or a spiritual version of that religion over the other. India with its diverse collection of religions is an apt example where atrocities in the name of religion and spiritual dogmas are committed on a regular basis. Even if a victim does not suffer physical damage as a result, his or her own inability to make life decisions because of the dominance of spiritual elites is in itself a type of violence that hampers individual level growth.

Cultural Violence

Cultural violence occurs when a person is harmed as a result of practices that are part of his or her culture, religion or tradition. Cultural violence includes, but is not limited to:

- *Committing "honour" or other crimes against women.* In some parts of the world, women especially are susceptible to be physically harmed, shunned, maimed or killed in the name of honour. This idea of honour is actually a cultural construct where the woman is simultaneously considered the epitome of virtue and source of familial pride, and also a source of danger as she can very easily bring shame. Women thus come to be in a very vulnerable position where they have to be in constant vigilance of their self in order to remain safe even at the basic level of survival. It is obvious that an individual who needs to be constantly on guard cannot grow at an individual level and this is why the idea of honour and existence of honour killings in a society need to be stopped completely as it obstructs all women from challenging themselves to reach new heights.

- *Infidelity; committing adultery.* While honor killings are subjected to women who have committed or are accused of committing infidelity and adultery, at the other end of the spectrum we have the men who do not have to face prosecution when they commit the same acts. There has to start a realization that infidelity and adultery have a deep impact on the partner (no matter the gender) and creates conflict within the household. If the primary location of socialization is not conflict-free, one cannot expect that the household members will be able to become fully functional members of society.
- *Being raped.* While rape is a felony and punishable by most laws of the world, the loopholes at a cultural level make the position of women very low in society. In India, for example, many acts of rape do not get reported simply due to the ostracization that the rape victim faces in society. Not only are they viewed as "damaged property", in many occasions they face the brunt of honour killings as they are supposed to have brought shame to the family simply by being raped against their will. In order for women to grow in society, one needs to realize the terrible position they live in where they not only face the physical, emotional and psychological impact of being raped, but also, instead of being given justice, they are contrarily made to experience further cultural violence.

Verbal Abuse

Verbal abuse occurs when someone uses language, whether spoken or written, to cause harm to a person. Verbal abuse includes, but is not limited to:

- *Name-calling, insulting, and swearing.* We have gone through these examples in previous paragraphs.
- *Yelling.* There cannot but be a negative impact on the part of the listener if information is not imparted in a soothing or encouraging manner. This is a basic rule in organisations and institutions where methods of communication between those in power and those who are subordinates state that a stern voice is not equivalent to yelling. Even in everyday experience, especially when interacting with strangers, yelling gives an impression that the victim belongs in the lower sections of society's stratification. If a victim faces yelling on a regular basis, this leads to harming of his or her self-worth, and thus severely limiting their aspirations or start doubts in their ability to reach their potential.
- *Expressing negative expectations.* As we have discussed on numerous occasion before, every individual, by virtue of being part of society, feels the constant need to be accepted by others. In his or her search for acceptance, they inadvertently develop dependency on certain individuals, beginning with parents or patriarchal figures in the household. It then becomes the responsibility of these authority figures to mould their wards in the best way possible and expressing negative expectations is a counter to that. Not only do these verbal abuses stunt the wards' growth but also develop their anti- social tendencies.
- *Expressing distrust.* Similar to the example above, individuals need to feel self-worth through interactions with authority figures. In order to be taken seriously as a socially productive adult, individuals need constant reiteration of their abilities. While showing trust towards them yields positive results, the opposite happens when they are made to feel insecure by verbally making it known that they are not trustworthy enough.

- *Threatening violence against a person or his or her family members.* We have discussed the importance of primary socialization in the preceding paragraphs. It is but natural that the setting becomes a safe haven for an individual socially and emotionally. Verbal abuse that includes threat to the person or his or her family is therefore a combination of the various types of violence that we have mentioned before and is a huge blow to the security of an individual. Moreover, without this security, an individual will seldom have the opportunity or the drive to make improvements in personal growth.

It is appropriate that a small note be made here for the continued existence of sanctioned violence or the loopholes where it thrives. Now-a-day's violence against women and girls is a major problem. At least one in five of the world's female population has been physically or sexually abused by a man or men at in and outside home as well as work place also. From the above discussion on different kinds and theories of violence it is clearly observed that girls are facing so many problems in and outside the school system. A number of researches have been done on the violence against girls. So it is felt need to search about the researches which has been done in this field to overcome the problem. The second chapter is dealing with the review of related literature.

2
Review of Existing Literature

2.1 Review of Existing Literature

Every research project should be based on relevant thinking and researches that has preceded it. When completed, it becomes part of the accumulated knowledge in the field and so contributes to the thinking and researches that follow for any specific project to occupy in the development of a discipline, the research must be familiar with both previous theories and researches.

In research, the review of the literature serves as variety of background functions preparatory to the actual collection of data. In research approaches, the literature is reviewed to create the context from the past for the new study to be conducted with new subjects and newly obtained data. Reviewing the literature of related field gives a comprehensive and in-depth knowledge about the trend of research and quantum of work done in the concerned field of research critical survey of the particular research area point out the existing gaps and lacunas in it. Also it prevents the repetition of researches. Impressing on the need of related literature Good *el al.* (1954) stated, "The competent physician must keep constantly abreast to locate the information pertinent to the case in hand. Obviously, the careful investigator should become familiar with location and use of Sources of Educational information."

2.2 Reviews on Girl-specific Violence

Boyer, Wanda (2008) conducted a study entitled "Girl-to-Girl Violence: The Voice of the Victims"in which School violence is not gender-exclusive to boys; girls are also capable of violence. Research shows that girl-to-girl violence stems from competition for male attention and tends to be relational in nature, which typically takes the form of social alienation, spreading of rumours, and otherwise manipulating the victim's peer group. By proactively examining when—and under what conditions-various forms of aggression emerge in girl-to-girl violence, and by exploring the effects of the violence on victims, this article seeks to sensitize pre-adolescent girls, families, teachers, counsellors, and administrators about girl-to-girl violence prevention and cessation. Some prior literature on girls and boys who are victims has included classification of victims and the negative effects of victimization. However, it is telling that most of the prior literature on girl-to-girl violence is based on the perspective of the perpetrator. The purpose of this article is to sensitively examine the point of view of the primary and secondary victims, rather than "relegate them to the realms of subjectivism." Although pre-adolescent girls with a strong sense of personal identity, self-worth, and a respect for others typically do not engage in violent behaviour, the question is whether they become victims of school violence. What is the trajectory of victimization in girl-to-girl violence for both primary and secondary victims? To better frame a context for answering these questions, the author examined a case of victimization that began in pre-adolescence and extended over the course of the primary victim's grade 7 school year. It was only in grade 9, at the age of 14 that she felt able to discuss her perceptions of what happened to her. The author also obtained the perceptions of her family members as secondary victims.

Miller *et al.* (2009) conducted a study entitled "Parent and Peer Predictors of Physical Dating Violence Perpetration in Early Adolescence: Tests of Moderation and Gender Differences".This study examined parenting and peer predictors of physical dating violence perpetration during early adolescence and tested moderation among these predictors and gender. Participants were 2,824 ethnically diverse sixth-grade students with a recent boyfriend/girlfriend who was part of a multisite, longitudinal investigation of the development and prevention of violence among middle school students. Those students who reported having a boyfriend/girlfriend reported significantly more drug use and delinquent activity and were more likely to be male. Twenty-nine per cent of youth with a boyfriend/girlfriend reported perpetrating physical aggression against their boyfriend/girlfriend. Parenting and peer variables were significant predictors of physical dating violence. However, gender moderated the association between parenting practices and physical dating violence, with parental monitoring inversely linked to dating violence for boys and parent support for non-aggression inversely linked to dating violence for girls. Parents support for aggression also moderated the association between peer deviancy and reported perpetration. Finally, gender moderated the interaction between peer deviancy and parent support for non-aggressive solutions.

Susana (2003) views that women's organizations have created a paradigm shift in understanding and acting to end violence against girls and women. Where gender-based violence was once confined to whispers and silent suffering, it is now part of the public agenda. Women's groups and networks have insisted that violence against women is not only a crime; it is a violation of women's human rights. Rape, as an example, is not an "affront to a woman's chastity" but rather a profound violation of her bodily integrity and her right to dignity, security, and freedom from discrimination. She examines a recent assessment of initiatives to end violence against women that was conducted in 2002 by the United Nations Development Fund for Women (UNIFEM) and connected to current research, advocacy, and antiviolence organizing. She cited several examples from international societies such as cases of stove burning in Pakistan, date rape in the United States, acid throwing in Bangladesh, dowry deaths in India, so called honour killings in some parts of the Middle East and South Asia, female genital mutilation in Africa and the Middle East.

The social and economic consequences of gender-based violence are far-reaching and keep women from freely and wholly contributing to the social, economic, and political development of their communities. The first shelter in Latin America and the Caribbean, for "battered women" (the term most frequently used during early organizing efforts) was the Julia Burgos Protected House in Puerto Rico, established in 1979. Soon after, women's groups in Puerto Rico formed the Puerto Rican Coalition against Domestic Violence. In 1981, the first Latin American and Caribbean Feminist Encounter declared the 25th of November an International Day for No Violence against Women. By 1987, the government officially recognized the date as a day of commemoration in Puerto Rico.

The regional reports in UNIFEM's assessment repeatedly illustrated (*ibid*) stressing that violence against women is a human rights violation has moved the anti-violence agenda forwarded in many ways: First, it has provided a powerful lens that shifts the focus on violence against women from a private to a public matter. In so doing, it has added greater credibility to activists' claims and established a common language. Second, it has offered an opportunity to anchor and build global and regional networks. Third, it presents a methodology for determining government obligations. Under human rights law, for example, states are required to act with due diligence to address and end violence against women.

Leela Visaria (2000) found that dowry related violence leads to low self-esteem among Indian girls which contributes to women accepting beatings at the hands of their husbands. Like Miller (1992), she understands male patriarchy in terms of honour and claim over women as property. It is the violation of such notions by women which is 'punished' by violence (Hassan 1995). She tries to understand how and why violence enters into the husband-wife relationship, why it continues over the years, and the real motives of the perpetrators of violence. Women in the study frequently attributed violence to proximate causes like 'mistakes' in running the household:

- Children cared for, meal preparation and taste, household, economic constraints (asking for money to run the household), 'answering back' and not being 'obedient',
- Condition worsens with age, level of education of wife, poverty.

There is a lack of support from natal homes; and outsiders not expected to intervene as a private domestic dispute and not a public disquiet (Mohanty, 2015:227). This leads to high tolerance for violence, and many people viewing violence as a woman's due.

Chris *et al.* (2007) conducted a study in inner-city areas where levels of criminal violence in the neighbourhoods were apparently high. The authors investigated the concept of the violence-resilient school. Some degree of association between the patterns of behaviour and school practices was found where schools with a wider range of well-connected practices seemed to have less difficult behaviour.

Michele *et al.* (2001) studied teenage girls' views and experiences of violence, carried out in Scotland and researched the ways in which girls conceptualize experience and use violence. The authors faced problems of conducting empirical research on girls and violence. They found that social and legal rules position young minors with few decision-making powers, and so accessing girls under involved gaining consent from adult gatekeepers, such as parents and teachers. Therefore, consent from girls themselves did not ensure certainty. In participating in the research, most girls were entering unfamiliar territory, of what was required of them, of what was entailed in 'research' and of each respective roles.

As Hammersley and Atkinson have noted, "It is hard to expect 'honesty' and 'frankness' while never being frank and honest about oneself." The girls showed more interest in the researchers' personal lives; and in the research setting, girls' accounts and definitions of violence were the result interaction with the researchers. The researchers had to balance their own interpretation of events with those of the participants like in relation to girls' definitions of what 'counted' as violence. Thus, a certain amount of interpretation of the girls' experience was needed.

Mizanur R. and M. Kabir (2006) find that the most common type of abuse to women worldwide is domestic violence. The legal systems discriminate against women and fail to protect them. In addition, economic structure, empowerment of women, cultural systems also contribute to gender-based violence.

Michelle (2011) concurs the view that domestic violence, in its various forms has a multifaceted relationship with the "stages of development" in developing countries such as India (See Bates *et al.*, 2004: 197; Nàved & Persson 2005: 299). There are a variety of data on Indian households, varying from state to state, villages to cities etc. There is a general understanding that more education and industrialisation leads to less violence. However, for example, if the Indian wives were to simultaneously begin paid-work (i.e. gain an income less household chores and therefore challenge the family power norm), this could be threat to the husband's power in the marriage and lead to physical violence. However, these states differ in different sites [Krishnan (2005), Verma and Collumbien (2003), Panda and Agarwal (2005)]. The author explores the possible consequences for women and development in India more generally:

1. Underlying patriarchal causes of violence against women (Dobash *et al.*, 1992; Mann, 2008), or
2. Structural inequalities and individual dynamics of violence perpetrated by both partners in the home (Dutton & Nicholls, 2005; Straus, 1991; Romans *et al.*, 2007), or,
3. Several authors such as Anderson (1997) and Heise (1998) attempted to bridge the gap by integrating the determinants of abuse. Anderson has suggested the addition of gendered components to family violence theories, resource theory. Heise (1998: 263) has proposed the adoption of an ecological framework. "Gender interacts with structures marital status, and socio-economic status to influence power within relationships propensities for domestic violence" (Anderson 1997 : 667).

In India, the historical, underlying patriarchal system dominates the domestic violence discourse. Recently, industrialisation and economic development have occurred and as expected, gender role changes have been assimilated with varying degrees of resistance. However, though severe beatings are to be publicly and legally condemned, the vast majority of domestic violence is deemed a husband's right, or accepted as an inevitable part of married life.

2.3 Reviews on Sexual Violence

Abuya *et al.* (2012) found that 31 per cent of young Kenyan women of ages 15-24 reported sexual harassment and violence (SHV), with a majority experiencing sexual debut due to coercion (Central Bureau of Statistics, 2004). Data were obtained from a sample of 20 girls attending school in Kamu and Lafamu (pseudonyms used for the study sites), 10 girls who had dropped out of school, and 14 teachers, using structured interviews. A phenomenological approach was used to describe narratives of girls' experiences with SHV in and out of school. The findings indicated that girls experienced frequent SHV in and out of school despite the Sexual Offences Act enacted by the Kenyan Parliament in 2006. Hence, stakeholders need to reengage and implement existing policies on sexual abuse among children and women.

Alam *et al.* (2009) explained the extent and type of sexually harassing behaviour or intimidations unmarried adolescent girls experienced on their way to school, college or social visits and type of perpetrators in victims' view in rural Bangladesh using data of the 2004 National Nutrition Programme baseline survey. The survey collected self-reported data on sexual harassments of 5,106 girls aged 13-19 years selected randomly. Results reveal that gendered harassments were experienced by 35 per cent of the girls, unwanted sexual attentions by 34 per cent, and sexual intimidations by 14 per cent, yielding prevalence of sexual harassments of any type 43 per cent. Higher girls' education and household economic status heightened their risks of being harassed. Perpetrators were male young spoilt bullies (64%), neighbourhood youth (30%), students (22%) and hoodlums (6%). High prevalence of sexual harassments mirrors vulnerability of adolescent girls in the community and deserves to be tackled to achieve millennium development goals (MDGs) in gender equality in health and social development.

Bhana, Deevia (2012) conducted a study on township girls in South Africa and showed enduring experiences of sexual violence both in and out of the school. Fear of boys and men were articulated in relation to boyfriends, male teachers, men in the township neighbourhood and men in the home. While the girls attempted to exercise agency in arresting their fears, these appeared to be too limited in the context of great structural and social inequalities and the pervasiveness of gender norms through which male sexual violence is asserted. The implication for increasing girls' exercise of agency is raised as a human rights issue.

Camacho *et al.* (2012) examined the quality of peer relations as a mediator between exposure to IPV (intimate partner violence) and internalizing behaviours in a sample of 129 preadolescents and adolescents (age 10-18), who were interviewed *via* telephone as part of a multigenerational, prospective, longitudinal study. Relational victimization is also examined as a moderator of IPV exposure on internalizing behaviours. Results demonstrate a significant association of exposure to severe IPV and internalizing behaviours. Relational victimization is found to moderate the effects of exposure to severe IPV on internalizing behaviours. Their findings suggest that the effects of exposure to IPV had a particularly important effect on the risk for internalizing problems if the adolescent "also" experienced relational victimization.

Gadin's study **(2012)** was to enhance the understanding of young girls' experiences of peer sexual harassment in elementary school and of normalizing processes of school-related sexualized violence. Six focus group interviews with girls in Grade 1 through 6 were carried out in an elementary school in the northern part of Sweden. Content analyses showed that young girls experienced verbal, non-verbal, and sexual assault behaviours at school. Sexual harassment as a concealed phenomenon and manifest within a romantic discourse were themes found in the analysis. She found that schools have to acknowledge behaviours related to sexual harassment as a potential problem even in young ages and develop methods to approach the subject also for this age group.

Hamelin *et al.* (2010) addressed the long-term consequences of adverse childhood experiences among women in Oceania, in particular among indigenous women. They aimed to report prevalence's of childhood sexual abuse (CSA) and to assess the negative sexual health consequences in adulthood by comparing indigenous Kanak to non-Kanak women in New Caledonia. Data come from a population survey on violence against women and health. Face-to-face interviews were conducted in 2002-03 with adult women randomly selected from the electoral list. Separate models for Kanak (n = 329) and non-Kanak women (n = 426) were performed. Regression models adjusted for relevant socio-demographic factors were conducted to estimate the odds ratios for the associations between childhood sexual abuse and adult sexual health outcomes. A non-significant difference between Kanak (11.8%) and non-Kanak women (14.4%) was found for the prevalence of CSA. Among Kanak women, CSA increases the risk of sexually transmitted infections, of non-desired sexual intercourse with an intimate partner and of experience of adult sexual violence. However, use of modern contraception as an adult was more frequent among CSA Kanak victims, as compared to other Kanak women. Among non-Kanak women, only abortion appeared significantly associated with CSA. Thus, the findings show that in all ethnic communities of New Caledonia, a history of child sexual abuse is not rare among women. They also shed light on the long-term consequences of CSA, suggesting that the effect of CSA may differ according to ethnic membership and subsequent social stratification and gender norms. Efforts to break the silence around violence against girls and establish a stronger foundation are required in New Caledonia. Prevention programmes on violence against women and sexual health that take into account the cultural and social heterogeneity are needed.

Orpinas *et al.* (2013) argued that although research on dating violence is growing, little is known about the distinct developmental trajectories of dating violence during adolescence. The current study identified trajectories of physical dating violence victimization and perpetration that boys and girls follow from sixth to twelfth grade, examined the overlap of these trajectories, and characterizes them by perceptions of a caring dating relationship and acceptability of dating aggression. The sample consisted of randomly selected sixth graders from nine schools in Northeast Georgia (n = 588; 52 % boys; 49 % White, 36 % African American, 12% Latino) who completed yearly surveys from Grades 6-12. The latent class mixture modelling was used to identify the trajectories and generalized estimating equation models to examine the acceptability of dating aggression by dating violence trajectories. Participants followed two trajectories of dating violence victimization (boys: low and high; girls: low and increasing) and two of perpetration (boys and girls: low and increasing). When examining the joint trajectories of victimization and perpetration, a similar proportion of boys (62 %) and girls (65 %) were in the low victimization and low perpetration group and reported the lowest acceptance of dating aggression. The same proportion of boys and girls (27 %) were in the high/increasing victimization and perpetration group, and reported the highest acceptance of dating aggression. However, acceptance of dating aggression decreased from Grade 6-12 for all groups, even for those whose trajectory of dating violence increased. Victimization and perpetration were associated with reporting a less caring dating relationship. Results highlight the importance of focusing prevention efforts early for adolescents who follow this increasing probability of physical dating violence.

Reeve, and Pamela (2012) conducted a study entitled "*Dating Norms and Dating Violence among Ninth Graders in Northeast Georgia: Reports from Student Surveys and Focus Groups*'. This mixed-method study describing the norms supporting male-to-female and female-to-male dating violence in a diverse sample of ninth graders. The quantitative study, based on student surveys (n = 624), compared norms supporting dating violence by sex, race/ethnicity, and dating status, and it examined the relation between dating violence norms and physical aggression and victimization. The qualitative study, based on 12 focus groups, explored participants' views of dating aggression. Findings revealed more support for female-to-male aggression, greater acceptance of norms supporting dating violence by non-White students, a strong association between norms and physical aggression but only in males, and a high correlation between victimization and perpetration. Participants rejected male-to-female dating aggression because of peer pressure not to hit girls, parents' beliefs that denounce dating violence, the superior physical advantage of boys over girls, and legal consequences. Results highlight the importance of culturally sensitive and gender-specific interventions.

Shen *et al.* (2012) conducted a study entitled *"Predictors of Dating Violence among Chinese Adolescents: The Role of Gender—Role Beliefs and Justification of Violence"*. In Chinese societies, violence among adolescent dating partners remains a largely ignored and invisible phenomenon. The goal of this study was to examine the relationships among gender-role beliefs, attitudes justifying dating violence, and the experiences of dating-violence perpetration and victimization among Chinese adolescents. This study has used self-reporting measures to collect data from a probability sample of 976 adolescents (mean age = 15.9) in three Chinese societies: Taiwan, Hong Kong, and Shanghai. Research results reveal a high prevalence of dating violence (including physical violence, sexual violence, and controlling behaviour) among

Chinese adolescents with dating experience: the perpetration rate is 27.3 per cent and the victimization rate is 39 per cent. Study results demonstrate that adolescents who endorse traditional gender-role beliefs tend to view dating violence as acceptable behaviour. Boys' endorsement of traditional gender roles, boys' attitudes justifying boy-on-girl violence, and boys' attitudes against girl-on-boy violence predict boys' actual sexual-violence behaviour. Moreover, boys' attitudes justifying boy-on-girl dating violence is the strongest predictor of boys' perpetration of physical and sexual dating violence. This study also shows that boys' hostility is a significant predictor of boys' controlling behaviour. Programmes for preventing dating violence should include components designed to challenge traditional gender-role beliefs and attitudes justifying dating violence.

Sears *et al.* (2007) examined the co-occurrence of and risk factors for adolescent boys' and girls' self-reported use of psychologically, physically, and sexually abusive behaviours in their dating relationships. The participants were 324 boys and 309 girls in grades 7, 9, or 11 who completed surveys at school. Descriptive analyses showed that 19 per cent of boys and 26 per cent of girls reported having used two or more forms of dating violence. One-third of students in grade 7 had already used at least one form of aggressive behaviour in this context. Canonical correlation analyses indicated that boys' and girls' use of multiple forms of dating violence were predicted by their attitudes towards and experiences with violence. After controlling for general abusiveness, boys' use of sexually abusive behaviour and girls' use of psychologically abusive behaviour were linked to specific risk factors that suggest an enactment of social scripts associated with their respective gender roles.

Swahn *et al.* (2008) examined sex differences in the patterns of repeated perpetration and victimization of physical violence and psychological aggression within dating relationships and same-sex peer relationships. Data were obtained from the Youth Violence Survey: Linkages among Different Forms of Violence, conducted in 2004, and administered to all public school students enrolled in grades 7, 9, 11 and 12 (N = 4,131) in a high-risk school district. Analyses of adolescents who dated in the past year (n = 2,888) show that girls are significantly more likely than boys to report physical violence and psychological aggression perpetration within dating relationships. However, boys are significantly more likely than girls to report physically injuring a date. Boys are also significantly more likely than girls to report physical violence victimization and perpetration within same-sex peer relationships. Implications and directions for future research are discussed.

Tora, Abebayehu (2013) conducted a study entitled *"Assessment of Sexual Violence against Female Students in Wolaita Sodo University, Southern Ethiopia"*. Studies indicate that girls and women encounter sexual violence in their day-to-day social life in all cultures and societies. This study aimed to determine the prevalence of sexual violence against female students in Wolaita Sodo University and Reported level of these perpetrations was experienced mainly at high school and during enrolment year in the university. Boy friends, close friends, family members and relatives, school and university teachers, other employees, and strangers were found to be the key perpetrators of sexual violence against women. Interventions are required to create a safe learning environment for female students through prevention and rehabilitation programmes.

Nancy and Donald (2006) examine the nature of media coverage of sexual violence against women and girls in Jamaica and the impact it has on women's life in general. Albert Bandura's (1986) social learning theory (SLT) states that personal factors, environmental influences, and behaviour continually interact. The violence situation could be associated with the lack of self-efficacy often linked with a variety of factors, including gender inequality and the lack of skills often associated with environmental and societal factors like lack of societal support for change. To achieve self-directed change, people need to be given not only the reason to alter risky habits, but also the behavioural means, resources, and social support to do so. Imitation and identification to explain how people learn certain behaviours and practices through observation of others in their environment. Biological determinism theorists associate violence to testosterone and physical power thus explaining why males are more prone to instigating violence against women (Humm, 1989; Wood, 2001). Feminist scholars have however gone beyond biological explanations to include social and cultural factors as key contributors of violence against women. Nancy Chodorow (2002) for example sees a complex link between violence/aggression and gender, arguing that violence is tied in some way to nationalism and its equivalents (tribal, ethnic, racial) witnessed throughout history. Cultural ideologies thus come into factor where behaviours re-establish traditional male dominancy and symbolically put women back in their place. Katz (2003) also argues that physical size and strength and the ability to use violence successfully remains one of the areas that masculine power is attainable, particularly among men who experience unsettling changes in their lives.

Maithreyi K conducted a study entitled "*Understanding Violence against Wome*n". Violence may be visible, invisible, or camouflaged and used to uphold cultural codes of honour. In the case of marital rape, the women face inability to make decisions regarding their own bodies; and invest the victims with guilt about their "mistakes" in not sufficiently honouring their expected duties to husband and in- laws.

2.4 Reviews on Emotional and Psychological Violence

Eisman *et al.* (2015). Depression is a serious mental health concern among adolescents. Violence exposure is a potent risk factor for depression. Social support may help reduce depression risk, even when adolescents are exposed to violence. Using a compensatory model of resilience, we investigated the influence of violence exposure and social support on depression over time in a sample of urban youth during the high school years. The results support a compensatory model of resilience. Promoting positive parent-child communication among urban youth living in disadvantaged contexts may help reduce the probability that exposure to violence will result in depressive symptoms. *School* exclusion and violence are defined with boys as the reference point and relatively little attention is given to the various forms of exclusion—disciplinary exclusion, self-exclusion and withdrawal from learning—to which girls are subject.

Osler (2006). Girls in difficulty at school receive less attention than their male peers from policy-makers, teachers and researchers. They find it more difficult to access resources. The concept of exclusion needs to be expanded to encompass girls' experiences.

Rothon *et al.* (2011) investigated the extent to which social support can have a buffering effect against the potentially adverse consequences of bullying on school achievement and mental health. It uses a representative multi-ethnic sample of adolescents attending East London secondary schools in three boroughs. Bullied adolescents were less likely to achieve the appropriate academic achievement benchmark for their age group and bullied boys (but not girls) were more likely to exhibit depressive symptoms compared to those not bullied. High levels of social support from family were important in promoting good mental health. There was evidence that high levels of support from friends and moderate (but not high) family support was able to protect bullied adolescents from poor academic achievement. Support from friends and family was not sufficient to protect adolescents against mental health difficulties that they might face as a result of being bullied. More active intervention from schools is recommended.

McKelvey *et al.* (2011) examined the moderating effects of family conflict and gender on the relationship between community violence and psychosocial development at age 18. The study sample consisted of 728 children and families who were part of the Infant Health and Development Programme study of low-birth-weight, pre-term infants. In this sample, adolescent psychosocial outcomes were predicted by community violence differently for male and female children and based on their experiences of conflict at home. For male children, being in a "high" conflict family as a child exacerbated the negative effects of community violence such that internalizing problems (depression and anxiety) and risk-taking behaviours increased as community violence increased, while being in a "low" conflict family protected the child against the negative impacts of the community. For female adolescents, there were no moderating effects of family conflict on the relationship between community violence and externalizing problems. Moderating effects for internalizing problems demonstrated that being in "low" conflict families did not serve as protection against community violence for girls as was demonstrated for boys. These findings demonstrate the long-term effects of community violence on child development, highlighting the importance of gender and family context in the development of internalizing and externalizing problems.

Caracci (2003) argued that violence against women has emerged as a major public health and human rights issue at the international level. In addition to violence from an intimate partner, women can be victims of several forms of violence and coercion. The physical and mental health consequences as well as the costs to society are enormous. This article reviews the scope of the problem, the emotional consequences, the cultural context in which violence is perpetrated and condoned, the spread of HIV as a consequence of violence, and the barriers to our understanding that still exist in the field. Moreover, this review focuses on the work of the United Nations to raise awareness and promote action on this human rights violation at the international level. In particular, the work of the World Health Organization has brought significant advancements in our understanding of the phenomenon. Non-governmental organizations (NGOs) play an important role in addressing the issue by bringing it the attention of international bodies and making sure that resolutions are complied with. NGOs also help to monitor the implementation of programmes at the local level. While a great more remains to be done, the progress made over the past thirty years provides much hope that this pressing social and human rights issue will be appropriately addressed in the near future. This article reviews the scope of the problem, the emotional consequences, the cultural context in which violence is perpetrated and condoned, the spread of HIV as a consequence of violence, and the barriers to our understanding that still exist in the field.

Vacha Kishori Project Team (2002) conducted a study entitled *"Pre-adolescent Girls in Municipal Schools in Mumbai"*, The article is based on a study on school education in the urban situation and stresses on the importance of education in providing security. By tackling the issues of menstrual hygiene and menstrual taboos, it is found that women are kept under pressure all through their lives.

Impact of Violence

Ji-Kang and Hsi-Sheng (2011) conducted a study entitled "*The Impact of School Violence on Self-Esteem and Depression among Taiwanese Junior High School Students*". The majority of research on the outcome of school violence has been conducted in Western countries. Empirical studies on how school violence impacts student psychological well-being in a Chinese cultural context are relatively limited. The aim of this study was to address this gap by exploring how student maltreatment by teachers, student perpetration against students, and student victimization by other students affected the self-esteem and depression of 1,376 junior high school students in Taiwan. This study also explored how gender, family socio-economic status (SES), student-teacher relationships and peer support moderate the impact of school violence. Structural equation analyses showed that student victimization by students and student perpetration of violence against students successfully predicted depression, but not self-esteem. Student maltreatment by teachers was associated with neither depression nor self-esteem.

Sibnath and Kerryann (2012) sought to understand the pervasiveness and impact of physical, psychological, and sexual violence on the social adjustment of Grade 8 and 9 school children in the state of Tripura, India. The study participants, 160 boys and 160 girls, were randomly selected from classes in eight English and Bengali medium schools in Agartala city, Tripura. Data were collected using a self-administered Semi-structured Questionnaire for Children/ Students and a Social Adjustment Inventory which was custom-made for the study based on measures to the extant research adapted in the Indian context. Findings revealed that students experienced physical (21.9%), psychological (20.9%), and sexual (18.1%) violence at home, and 29.7 per cent of the children had witnessed family violence. Boys were more often victims of physical and psychological violence while girls were more often victims of sexual violence. The social adjustment scores of school children who experienced violence, regardless of the nature of the violence, was significantly lower when compared with scores of those who had not experienced violence (p less than 0.001). Social adjustment was poorer for girls than boys (p less than 0.001). The study speaks in favour of early detection and intervention for all child maltreatment subtypes and for children exposed to inter-parental violence, and highlights the crucial role of schools and school psychology in addressing the problem.

Violence exposure within each setting of community, school, or home has been linked with internalizing and externalizing problems.

Although many children experience violence in multiple contexts, the effects of such cross-contextual exposure have not been studied. A study by **Sylvie and Windle (2010)** addresses this gap by examining independent and interactive effects of witnessing violence and victimization in the community, home, and school on subsequent internalizing and externalizing problems in early adolescence. A community sample of 603 boys and girls (78% African American, 20% Caucasian) participated in a longitudinal study of youth violence. During two assessments 16 months apart, adolescents reported on witnessing violence and victimization in the community, school, and home, and their internalizing and externalizing problems. Multiple regressions tested the independent and interactive effects of witnessing violence or victimization across contexts on subsequent adjustment, after controlling for initial levels of internalizing and externalizing problems and demographic covariates. Witnessing violence at school predicted anxiety and depression; witnessing at home was related to anxiety and aggression; and witnessing community violence predicted delinquency. Victimization at home was related to subsequent anxiety, depression, and aggression; victimization at school predicted anxiety; and victimization in the community was not independently related to any outcomes. Finally, witnessing violence at home was associated with more anxiety, delinquency, and aggression only if adolescents reported no exposure to community violence. To them violence exposure at home and school had the strongest independent effects on internalizing and externalizing outcomes. Witnessing community violence attenuated the effects of witnessing home violence on anxiety and externalizing problems, perhaps due to desensitization or different norms or expectations regarding violence. However, no comparable attenuation effects were observed for victimization across contexts.

Mykota and Adele (2015) went on to argue that violence exposure is a serious public health concern for adolescents in schools today. Violence exposure can be quite severe and frequent with multiple acts of indirect and direct victimization having lasting effects on the physical, emotional, and intellectual well-being of adolescents. The purpose of the present study was to examine the rates of violence exposure and the relative risk for multiple exposures among adolescent youth living in rural communities. Results confirm that adolescents who live in rural areas were frequent victims of violence exposure and that males were more likely to be the victims than females. Moreover, the relative risk for multiple exposures either indirectly, directly, or in combination reveal that in all instances amplification of risk occurs. The study was an important first step in understanding the rates of violence exposure and victimization experienced by adolescent youth in rural Canada with implications for school-based programming presented.

2.5 Reviews on Causes of Violence and Rights/Prevention of the Child

Cameron *et al.* (2005) examined perceptions of the causes and nature of conflicts and violence among African-American girls in an urban high school. In-depth, iterative interviewing was used to explore the perceptions of these girls, male students, teachers, and other school personnel. Ethnographic observation was also used. Conflicts and violence among girls were produced by an insult or accusation made by one girl against another which by group norms required a commensurately aggressive response. Peers actively pressured girls to fight and those that did not were scapegoated by others. However, a mediation service was used by girls to end conflicts successfully.

Khoury-Kassabri *et al.* (2009) present the prevalence of students' reports of perpetration of violence toward peers and teachers among 16,604 7th through 11th grade Jewish and Arab students in Israel and examines the individual and school contextual factors that explain students' violence. The study explores how students' reports of violence are influenced by individual factors (gender, age, perception of school climate and intervention) and school contextual factors (cultural affiliation, SES of students' families, school and class size, school climate, intervention). Almost one-third of all students reported at least one form of perpetration towards peers, and one in five reported perpetration against teachers. Compared to the school climate characteristics, school organizational factors, and cultural affiliation, students' SES has the highest contribution to explained variance in reports of violence toward others. The discussion highlights the need to allocate more resources to schools in low-SES contexts to protect low-SES students from school violence.

Benninger-Budel's (2000) reported to the United Nations Committee on the Rights of the Child contains observations of the World Organisation Against Torture (OMCT) concerning the application of the U.N. Convention on the Rights of the Child by the nation of South Africa. Noting that the Convention is the only "mainstream" human rights instrument that explicitly states the rights apply equally to female and male children, the report first provides observations and recommendations concerning violence against girls in South Africa. General observations in this area indicate that despite Government efforts at the legislative, policy, and awareness levels, there remain both in law and practice, discrimination against girls and conflict between the constitution and religious and customary laws which perpetuate harmful practices against girls. This section then examines: violence against girls in the family, including early marriages, bride prices, genital mutilation, and virginity testing; violence against women in the community, specifically rape, and trafficking and prostitution; and violence perpetrated by the state, noting emotional, physical, and sexual abuse of children in residential facilities such as prisons. The section then notes the discrepancies among these treaties and between common law and customary rulings with regard to the definition of the child. Constitutional and legislative provisions are then noted in the areas of—child protection against all forms of discrimination; best interests of the child; right to participation; freedom from torture, inhumane and degrading treatment or punishment; deprivation of liberty; sexual exploitation and abuse; child labour; refugees and asylum seeker children; and children in conflict with the law. The concluding section notes that while the government of South Africa has adopted several measures and introduced a number of amendments to fit domestic legislation to the U.N. Convention, there are still many gaps and contradictions at the legislative level, and several problems have arisen from the economic and social conditions of the country. Specific recommendations are offered.

Davidoff and Carolyn (2015) conducted a study entitled "*Raising Voices: Teaching Teen Girls to Speak Out*". Teaching artists know that many of the children they teach are being deprived of essential human experiences. Poverty, violence, and ineffective education have left them with little hope of emotional or material success, and a student's connection to an artist can change his or her life in little and big ways. Paula Davidoff and Carolyn Hunt are writers and teaching artists. Paula is a storyteller, and Carolyn is a theatre director. Since 2005, they have been co-directors of Girls Surviving, a programme in writing and performance they started for adolescent girls in Morristown, NJ. An arts workshop or residency can give a child new insights about school, about their community, and about themselves. However, when the project is finished and the artist moves on, the child's life resumes its normal course and often the opportunity for change has passed by. A programme like Girls Surviving effects lasting change because the teaching artists' goal is to build and sustain close working relationships with each other, with their students, and with their community to create an ongoing arts opportunity. A girl surviving offers experiences that nudge teen girls out of their silence. The programme encourages girls to see the world through many different lenses, to hear and understand different points of view so that, when they feel confident to raise their voices, they will speak with greater wisdom.

Killam *et al.* (2014) conducted a study entitled "*Violence Prevention in Middle School: A Preliminary Study*". Violence in schools continues reflecting violence within society. There is a growing need for violence prevention programmes within the schools that provide students with the skills needed to cope with interpersonal and relationship is-sues effectively. This study was conducted at a middle school and there were 345 middle school students (6th to 8th grade) who participated in the study. The students participated in a violence prevention programme. In this study, the researchers used a pre-test/post-test design and the results indicated that there were some changes in attitudes towards violence that occurred after the intervention.

Mann *et al.* (2015) investigated community and family factors that influence school efforts to reduce odds of group bullying behaviour and victimization. Multilevel logistic regression was used to analyze data from the 2009 Youth in Iceland population school survey (N = 7084, response rate: 83.5%, 50.8% girls). Parental support and time spent with parents were protective against group bullying behaviour while worsening relationships with teachers and disliking school increased the likelihood of such behaviour. Knowing kids in the area increased the likelihood of group bullying while intergenerational closure was a protective factor. Normlessness was consistently positively related to group bullying. We found no indication of higher-level relationships across the bullying models. Parental support was protective against victimization. Disliking school, intergenerational closure, and anomie/normlessness were strongly and negatively related to victimization. We found some indication of multilevel relationships for victimization. Their findings support efforts to increase family and community connection, closure, and support as a part of school-based intervention. These factors become more important as young people participate in or experience greater odds of group bullying behaviour and victimization.

A report to the United Nations Convention on the Rights of the Child (Naqvi, 2001) contains observations of the World Organisation Against Torture (OMCT) concerning the application of the Convention by Turkey and observations regarding violence against girls in Turkey. The report is presented in three major parts. Part 1 asserts that despite the considerable legal framework for protecting children's rights, there is adequate proof that there are serious deficiencies in Turkey's system of child protection. Observations and recommendations are made in the following areas: (1) definition of a child; (2) torture and other cruel, inhuman, or degrading treatment or punishment; and (3) children in conflict with the law. This part concludes with recommendations related to the discrimination of Kurdish children and girls, treatment of refugee children, torture, and the juvenile justice system. Part 2 focuses on violence against girls in Turkey. This second part details problems related to domestic violence, marital rape, crimes committed against females in the name of "honour" virginity testing, sexual violence, prostitution and trafficking in girls, and state-perpetrated violence against girls. This part concludes with recommendations related to each of the problems discussed. Part 3 provides a summary of observations and recommendations by the U.N. Committee on the Rights of the Child—Turkey, including those related to difficulties in implementation the Convention; civil rights and freedoms; family environment and alternative care; basic health and welfare; education, leisure, and cultural activities; and special protection measures.

Turkum, Ayse Sibel (2011) conducted a study entitled "*School Violence: To What Extent Do Perceptions of Problem Solving Skills Protect Adolescents?*" This study examined whether adolescents' perceptions of problem solving skills differ according to their sex, experiences of exposure to violence, age and grade, and the variables predicting their experiences of exposure to violence. Data were collected from 600 (298 females, 302 males) 14-19 year-old students attending various types of high schools in central Eskisehir. The Problem Solving Inventory and a questionnaire were used in the study. Findings of the study revealed that students' perceptions of problem solving skills do not change according to their sex and the place they are exposed to violence. Adolescents' perceptions of problem solving skills differ in accordance with the level of their exposure to violence; perception level of the problem solving skills of the students rarely exposed to violence is higher than that of the students exposed to violence occasionally or often. Perception level of the adolescents who are often exposed to violence does not change depending on their sex and age. The variables predicting adolescents' experiences of exposure to violence are listed as perceptions of problem solving skills, sex, grade, age, and school type. In conclusion, the adolescents' perceptions of problem solving skills are partially effective in protecting them against school violence. The place of the skills training programmes—particularly the ones that aimed at prevention of and protection from violence—in the content of counselling programmes was discussed.

Yavuzer, Y. & Gundogdu, R. (2012) conducted a study entitled "*Teachers' Responsibilities in Preventing School Violence: A Case Study in Turkey*". It is generally acknowledged that teachers play an important role in preventing or reducing violence in schools. The objectives of this study were: (a) to identify teachers' responsibilities in terms of preventing violence among school children and (b) to solicit teachers' views as what they have been doing in preventing violence. Sample for the study comprised 43 teachers from the different regions of Turkey. These teachers had followed an in-service training called "Crime and Prevention of Violence in Educational Institutions". The survey method was used to collect data. To analyse the data, frequency distribution was used and the data was turned into a table as a percentage. These teachers proposed many suggestions to school administrators as what could be done to prevent violence in schools. The results obtained show that these teachers were aware of their responsibilities in terms of preventing violence in schools. They seemed to have knowledge as to what could be done to prevent or reduce violence in schools; however, these ideas were not translated into action.

David G. Gil (1971) conducted a study entitled "*Violence against Children*" This America-based paper develops a definition and conceptual model of violence against children—including culturally sanctioned use of physical force in child rearing. Gil is against the general understandings of "deviant" which are the result of personal characteristics, failings, problems, maladjustment, or dysfunction. Whatever label is used, the source of all deviance is conceived to be in the individual or his primary group, his family, rather than in characteristics of the society. The somewhat sensational concern with individual cases of child abuse seems, at times, to have a quality of "scapegoating," for it enables the public to express self-righteous feelings of anger, disgust, resentment, and condemnation toward an individual abusing parent while the entire society is constantly guilty of massive acts of "societal abuse" of millions of children, about which relatively little is said, and even less has been done in recent decades. One has to avoid the limitations inherent in the foregoing assumptions concerning the "individual as source" of behavioural deviance which seems to derive from a politically "conservative" premise. One has to make intervention strategies aimed mainly at changing the disorders of individuals and the pathology of families, rather than aspects of the social context in which these "disordered" individuals and "pathological" families live.This interpretation of the causal context of child abuse is matched logically by intervention strategies aimed mainly at changing the disorders of individuals and the pathology of families, rather than aspects of the social context in which these "disordered" individuals and "pathological" families.

Hyder and Malik (2007) explored violence against children as a challenge in the developing world. The authors tackled the issue of health problems among children in Pakistan and found that a confluence of macro risk factors, such as poverty, poor legal protections, illiteracy, and unemployment, create an enabling environment for violence.

Boivin *et al.* (2012) aimed to understand the nature of the relationships between three forms of past victimizations (exposure to interparental violence in childhood, sexual harassment by peers since beginning of high school, prior experience of dating violence), physical dating violence perpetration by adolescents, and anger-hostility and emotional distress. The sample was composed of 1,259 high school students aged between 14 and 19 years who answered self-report questionnaires. Mediation analyses were conducted according to Baron and Kenny's approach. Logistic and linear regression analysis reveal that being victim of sexual harassment by peers and of dating violence are associated to physical dating violence perpetration *via* a partial mediating effect of hostility in girls. Contrary to results with girls, there is a complete mediating effect of emotional distress for boys. Results suggest that dating violence prevention and intervention strategies could be adapted according to gender and that sexual harassment should be addressed.

Boyer, Wanda (2010) conducted a study entitled "*Preadolescent Violence among Girls*" This research study explored preadolescent girl-to-girl violence based on the perceptions of the victim at 14 years of age and those of her family. Using a heuristic research design, this constant comparative analysis of multiple data sources found: (a) a clearly delineated progression of girl-to-girl violence, (b) blindness surrounding girl-to-girl violence in the responses of not only the victim's family but also the victim herself, and (c) proactive factors and strategies for early recognition and prevention of girl-to-girl violence. The implications based on these findings include examining when and under what conditions various forms of aggression emerged, alternative trajectories of victimization, and future research that can inform the prevention of girl-to-girl violence.

Teachers may not be trained on how to prevent or address school violence and/or may lack the skills necessary to provide adequate intervention strategies. The purpose of this study was to explore urban K-6 teachers' perceptions of school violence at one metropolitan school.The conceptual framework for this study was supported by Bronfenbrenner's nested ecological development theory, which characterizes violence as an interaction among several sub-systems, such as factors internal and external to the school. The research questions were related to urban K-6 teachers' perceptions and knowledge of school violence and obstacles that prevent them from addressing school violence. The focus of this qualitative case study was 6 teachers' perspectives on school violence including prevention and intervention methods. Audiotaped semi-structured interviews were transcribed and analyzed by comparing and contrasting emergent themes, with similar themes being combined as a method of data reduction. The main findings highlighted the significance of understanding teachers' perceptions that the school, community, and family play in addressing school violence. Key results indicated that the teachers lacked training to cope with school violence and felt that professional development opportunities should be a priority at the school and district levels to support teachers in the classroom. One conclusion is that this study may lead to a blueprint for safer schools to end acts of violence. Based on the findings, it is recommended that teachers be trained to learn coping skills to address school violence. Social change implications include providing professional development opportunities for teachers, parents, community members, and local educational agencies on school violence.

Bent (2013) concluded that as more girls enter school around the world, the question remains how to keep them in school. One of the biggest challenges that schoolgirls face today is violence in school and in school-related activities. Afghan refugee girls attend school in Varamin, Iran. The Iranian government, in cooperation with the United Nations Children's Fund (UNICEF), supports education for Afghan refugees through home schooling, informal education, and classes conducted in regular schools. School girls of all ages have reported a large number of instances of sexual harassment and assault, ranging from gender discrimination to rape, exploitation, and physical and psychological intimidation in school. School girls have noted that they have faced public shaming by school authorities due to their gender; much of this happens in countries where girls are discouraged from attending school. Adolescent girls have also noted that in schools with inadequate bathrooms and facilities, they are less likely to attend school during their menstrual cycles, if not drop out completely when their cycles begin.

Perpetrators of violence against girls in school range from teachers, parents, authority figures, and fellow students. But violence does not only happen in school, it also happens during school-related activities and in some cases, on the walk to and from school. Consequences of such violence range from unwanted pregnancies at an early age, poor academic performance, high dropout rates and absenteeism, and low self-esteem among girls. Thus, any school, in any country with violence against girls denies those girls the right to education; this is a direct infringement of their rights as defined in the Convention on the Elimination of All Forms of Discrimination against Women (CEDAW). Schools are expected to uphold the rights and dignity of all school girls.

Unfortunately, we also know that violence against girls in schools is highly underreported, misunderstood, and rarely addressed. The lack of reports comes from difficulty researching the issue and sociocultural barriers. In this context, researchers found that nearly half of all sexual assaults in schools were committed against girls under 16 years old, and girls as young as the age of six were found to be victims of rape. There must be efforts taken by the international community to ensure that schools are a safe place for girls.

One of these efforts can be providing material and monetary support for schools in countries where violence against school girls is common. In many developing countries, education at all levels is too expensive and supplies are low. Moreover, for many families, a girl's education is far less important than a girl's labour and wages in the household. It is, therefore, important for governments, grassroots organizations and NGOs to introduce initiatives that encourage girls' education while also providing economic support to mothers, families and girls—who might otherwise not receive an education.

Currently, there are a number of powerful, creative solutions being implemented to help solve the global crisis in girls' education. We encourage each and every one of them—but the bottom line is that girls' education must be a significant priority on the international agenda.

Gagne and Claudiane (2013) argued that the role of coping strategies (approach and avoidance) as a mediating factor between parental psychological violence and adolescent behaviour problems, both internalized and externalized, as well as the protective role of social support were examined separately for boys and girls. A group of 278 adolescents (mean age: 14.2) were recruited in three high schools located in low, moderate, and high socio-economic areas. Participants were in the seventh, eighth, and ninth grades and each completed a self-administered questionnaire. The use of avoidant coping strategies partially mediated the link between parental psychological violence and behaviour problems among girls. The use of approach coping strategies partially mediated the link between parental psychological violence and behaviour problems among boys. In all cases, coping enhanced this link. No protective role of social support was found. On the contrary, this variable was found to increase the relationship between parental psychological violence and externalized behaviour problems among boys. These findings suggest that interventions aimed at strengthening coping skills and social support in adolescents may not be effective in alleviating various behavioural symptoms associated with parental psychological violence. They highlight the importance of prevention of psychologically violent parental practices, instead of only reacting to the problem after it has occurred.

Karagün (2015) attempted to determine the violence tendencies of young people studying in high school in terms of their participation in sports, status of exposure to violence and socio-demographic variables. It was also aimed to evaluate whether the identified violence tendency differed significantly by gender, grade, school success, features of the living place, parental education, economic level, doing sports or not, the ones doing sports regularly working being licensed or not, the number of years spent doing sports being licensed, the status of exposure to violence and the type of the violence exposure. To this end, 459 students in total, studying in 8 high schools randomly chosen within the boundaries of the district of Izmit of the province of Kocaeli in the academic year 2013 to 2014 and participating in the research voluntarily, were included in the scope of the study. As well as a survey determining the socio-demographic attributes, the Violence Tendency Scale developed by Haskan and Yildirim (2012) was administered to high school students. Consequently, it was found out that violence tendencies of young people differed significantly by gender, working in a sports branch being licensed, the number of years spent doing sports being licensed, the status of exposure to violence and the type of the violence exposure.

Bani (2014) investigated in secondary schools in the governorate of Mafraq. The aim was to identify the forms and causes of the phenomenon; hence to come out with the preventive and remedial measures, accordingly. The study was conducted in one of the secondary schools selected randomly in the city of Mafraq in the academic year 2013-14. To achieve the objectives of the study, the researcher used a qualitative case study methodology, drawing on the grounded theory model. The rationale of adopting this method was to generate forms, causes, and ways of preventing school violence as grounded in the data. Data were gathered through observations, interviews and documents. These data were broken down into themes. Themes were then grouped into categories. Common themes were then grouped together and links between them were identified. Both environmental factors and personal factors emerged as causes of school violence. Physical, and moral violence were found to be forms of this violence. The results showed that reducing and/or preventing school violence is a complex process which requires comprehensive educational programmes for all parties involved in the educational course. In light of the study results, the researcher proposed some preventive and remedial measures for the phenomenon.

Yan *et al.* (2010) examined the association between dating violence victimization and psychosocial risk and protective factors among Latino early adolescents. An anonymous, cross-sectional, self-reported survey was administered to a convenience sample of Latino youth (n = 322) aged 11 to 13 residing in suburban Washington, D.C. The dependent variable was physical dating violence; the independent variables included violence, substance use, emotional well-being, prosaically behaviours, and parenting practices. Multivariate logistic regression models were constructed and adjusted odds ratio and 95 per cent confidence interval were examined. Overall, 13.5 per cent (n = 43) of Latino early adolescents reported being a victim of physical dating violence within the past year. The prevalence was 14.4 per cent for girls and 12.9 per cent for boys. Among the girls, binge drinking was the sole risk behaviour associated with dating violence. Gun carrying, alcohol consumption, and having considered suicide were associated with dating violence among the boys. Physical dating violence appears to affect a small but significant proportion of Latino early adolescents and is associated with other risk behaviours. Healthy dating relationship programmes are warranted for middle school youth with some tailoring to reflect gender differences in risk profiles.

Although there have been surveys of what students of medicine (Coombs, 1968; Lief & Karlen, 1976), social work (Murphy, 1976) and nursing (Mace, Bannermann & Burton, 1974) are being taught about human sexuality, the comparable education of clinical psychology graduate students has never been assessed.No doubt motivated students in even these programmes can find relevant educational and training experiences outside the programmes' offerings, but nonetheless a subtle message about the peripheral importance (at best) or taboo nature (at worst) of sexuality is being conveyed by the programmes' inattention to sex education **(Sharon, 1986)**.

Malavika Karlekar (1998) conducted a study entitled "*Domestic Violence*". The ever-present fact of violence, both overt and covert physical and non-physical has an overwhelming on feminine identity formation. Using the life cycle approach this article argues that at every discrimination and violence, particularly against girl children and later women within the household, or conjugal. With age, problems are compounded with increased dependency, illness and fatigue. Ubiquity of violence against women, both within the home and in public spaces, the celebration experiences has led to the emergence of alternative discourses where the 'truth' and validity structures, norms and roles are called into question.

Violence has an overwhelming influence on feminine identity formation. Using the life cycle approach this article argues that women face discrimination and violence at every turn. Veena Das has commented in the context of Punjabi kinship, certain moral rules which influence the trajectory of individual lives (Das, 1976). It can be argued that these moral rules operate to maintain a certain gender-biased order internal to families and kinship systems.

2.6 A Global Comparison of Violence on Women and Girls

Now that we have gone through the types of violence, let us now concentrate upon violence particularly on women. Therefore, here under is presented a brief description based on different case studies: International Scenario, Indian Scenario and Mizoram Scenario.

International Scenario

Susana T. Fried (2003) examined a recent assessment of initiatives to end violence against women that was conducted in 2002 by the United Nations Development Fund for Women (UNIFEM) and finds that the social and economic consequences of gender-based violence are far-reaching and keeps women from freely and wholly contributing to the social, economic, and political development of their communities. She also finds that, "gender-based violence can be locally and culturally specific" and include, "stove burnings in Pakistan, date rape in the United States, acid throwing in Bangladesh, dowry deaths in India, so-called honour killings in some parts of the Middle East and South Asia, female genital mutilation in Africa and the Middle East" (2003: 99). She highlights UNIFEM's categorisation of violence against women as a human rights violation, and its role in moving forward an anti-violence agenda, "First, it has provided a powerful lens that shifts the focus on violence against women from a private to a public matter. In so doing, it has added greater credibility to activists' claims and established a common language. Second, it has offered an opportunity to anchor and build global and regional networks. Third, it presents a methodology for determining government obligations. Under human rights law, for example, states are required to act with due diligence to address and end violence against women."

A case study by **M. Mizanur Rahman and M. Kabir (2006)** reflects UNIFEM's agenda as it is found that the most common type of abuse to women worldwide is domestic violence, and particularly in Bangladesh, the legal systems discriminate against women and fail to protect them. Economic structure and cultural systems contribute to gender-based violence; and interestingly, such is true even in the case of empowerment of women which tends to shake the patriarchal *status quo*. Hassan (1995) shows that in Pakistani society, male patriarchy is weighed in terms of honour and claim over women as property. It is the violation of such notions by women which is 'punished' by violence.

Giovanni Caracci (2003) furthers the scope of the problem in terms of the effects of violence on women's physical, reproductive, and mental health, the relationship between violence and HIV infections, the cultural and contextual aspects of violence against women, and the barriers to understanding the phenomenon. Alexandra Arriaga (2002) brings to our attention the UN estimation that worldwide, females are biologically more susceptible to HIV/Aids, and this doesn't count needle exchange. Based on case study in Kenya and the sex ring in South Asia and Eastern Europe, she finds that discrimination is the root cause of all violence against women. Caracci finds that physical, sexual, and psychological abuse often overlap, and that abused women have consistently been found to function at a lower level than non-abused ones and prone to a high risk for suicide. The UN's 1985 World Conference in Nairobi is particularly important for being the first to declare violence against women as a major public issue and a *sine qua non* for the promotion of peace.

Nancy Muturi and Patricia Donald (2006) examine the nature of media coverage of sexual violence against women and girls in Jamaica and the impact it has on women's life in general; and surmise that female upliftment is possible only through professionalism in media as well as in NGOs where awareness and sensitisation is introduced to both sexes.

A case study by **Adnan Ali Hyder and Fauzia Aman Malik (2007)** based in Pakistan focuses upon violence against children and posits this as a challenge in the developing world where a confluence of macro risk factors, such as poverty, poor legal protections, illiteracy, and unemployment, create an enabling environment for violence. These causes also further complicate health problems.

The importance of schools in the perception and eradication of violence can be seen in the work of **Watkins *et al.* (2007)**. They found that in the UK, particularly in the inner-city areas where levels of criminal violence in the neighbourhoods were high, the corresponding schools would show resilience to violence solely based on the number of their "school practices". There was some degree of association between the patterns of behaviour and school practices, and schools with a wider range of well-connected practices relatively avoided difficult behaviour.

Indian Scenario

Domestic violence, in its various forms has a multifaceted relationship with the "stages of development" in developing countries such as India (Bates *et al.*, 2004: 197; Nàved & Persson 2005: 299). Michelle T. Hackett (2011) feels that in India, the historical underlying patriarchal system dominates the domestic violence discourse. Though severe beatings are be publicly and legally condemned, the vast majority of domestic violence is deemed a husband's right, or accepted as an inevitable part of married life. She moreover questions the assumption that domestic violence will wane as a society develops. Recently, industrialisation and economic development has led to changes in gender roles with varying degrees of resistance. But as Krishnan (2005), Verma & Collumbien (2003), and Panda & Agarwal (2005) have shown—there are varying statistics in various sites where the Indian wife faces physical violence if she begins paid work. This is because by doing so, household norms get challenged particularly in terms of household chores and taking care of the children; and the husband's power in the marriage gets threatened.

Vacha Kishor (2002) understands the importance of education in providing security to young girls. However, in her case study of schools in Mumbai, she witnesses the prominence of issues of menstrual hygiene and menstrual taboos. In this way schools are just another chapter of a woman's life where she is kept under pressure to act and behave in a certain manner.

Maithreyi Krishnaraj (2007) tackles the issue of violence that occurs to women in an invisible form. In India, violence is often camouflaged and used to uphold cultural codes of honour. Women find themselves in situations where they are unable to make decisions regarding their own bodies. Marital rape for example, invests the victim with guilt about her "mistakes" in not sufficiently honouring her expected duties to husband and in-laws. This kind of silence should not be confused as absence of violation. As Miller (1992) says, low self-esteem among Indian girls contributes to women accepting beatings at the hands of their husbands.

Accepting violence as repentance for "mistakes" is covered by Leela Visaria's (2000) work on domestic violence in rural Gujarat where she questions how and why violence enters into the husband-wife relationship, why it continues over the years, and the real motives of the perpetrators of violence. Besides dowry related violations, women in the study frequently attributed violence to causes like "mistakes" in running the household. Visaria found two important facets to the problem. One was the nature of these "mistakes" which range from—taking care of children, meal preparation and taste, economic constraints of the household (asking for money to run the household), 'answering back' and not being 'obedient', etc. The other facet was that these conditions worsen with age and poverty, and during all this there is lack of support from natal homes and outsiders are not expected to intervene in others' domestic affairs. In general there is a high tolerance for violence, and many view it as a woman's due.

Mizoram Scenario

In Mizoram, the prohibition and elimination of corporal punishment in schools was a priority in the 2005 and the 2007 National Plan of Action for Children. Corporal punishment was prohibited in 2009, although it remained legal in some states, and schools were provided with teacher guidelines to encourage 'positive engagement' with children. There is little evidence, however, that these policy reforms have eliminated corporal punishment. The unexpected violence that broke out left parents and students anxious, as they struggled to get home from school. With the situation getting out of control, schools and colleges had to be closed early. Around noon, institutions allowed students to go home. Some schools sent text messages to parents assuring them that the children could remain safe in school until the regular end of the working day. However, most parents rushed to schools to take their wards back home.

Taking into consideration all the aforementioned accounts, the situation in Mizoram seems to be comparatively harmonious as far as gender relations are concerned. Though we shall go into it in detail and with special consideration to girls at secondary schools, here are a few statistical findings based on the work by Mizoram State Child Protection

Society. We have broken down the state level annual Child Welfare Committee cases from 2012-2016 in particular reference to girls:

Table 2.1: Child Abuse Cases in Mizoram (2012-2016)

Sl. No.	Type of Abuse	2012	2016
1	Neglected	**33**	**59**
2	Sexually Abused	**19**	**72**
3	Physically Abused	**13**	**27**
4	Emotionally Abused	**03**	**15**
Total		**58**	**173**

The 2015-16 report was thorough in inclusion of the school sphere and only 12 girls reported physical abuse and 1 reported emotional abuse at the hands of teachers. In order to carry out the project in a wholesome manner a number of literatures have been reviewed in context to the project; and erstwhile case studies spanning across the world, and specifically ones related to India, have been used in a comparative methodology. The Mizo society in this manner has been found to have a relatively different scenario when it comes to the position of women, and by extension, the position of girls in school settings. A qualitative analysis has been made in this regard; and further hypotheses are proposed that the general social norms outside the school make a difference within the school.

2.7 Statement of the Problem

Violence is a major barrier to education for millions of girls across the globe. The prevalence of violence against girls affects both their rights to education and their rights in education. The Millennium Development Goals (MDGs), including Goal 2 (universal primary education) and Goal 3 (gender equality), make no explicit mention of violence against girls as a critical structural barrier to education (UN 2000). The issue has also been neglected by major education initiatives such as the Global Campaign for Education; Violence against girls is not a single phenomenon.—Violence or the fear of violence is an important reason for girls not attending school. Besides being in itself an infringement of girls' rights, violence is also denying girls their right to education.

Research on violence against girls, peer-to-peer sexual harassment during the past two decades has forced the researcher to see that schools may well be the training grounds for sexual and domestic violence through the practice of and permission given to the public performance of sexual harassment. Peer-to-peer sexual harassment is rampant in Secondary schools across the country. Yet, when educators and policy-makers consider interventions to curb youth violence, they usually overlook sexual and gender violence. This oversight occurs despite the growing recognition of the problems of teen dating violence, acquaintance/date rape, and bullying, hazing, battering and domestic violence. When gender violence is acknowledged in Secondary schools, staff members from sexual assault and domestic violence organizations are frequently asked to make classroom presentations on teen dating violence, date rape, battering, and sexual harassment. In order to provide effective interventions and prevention work on student-to-student sexual harassment and gender violence, researcher developed a research project that utilized a collaborative intervention model in order to develop a curriculum for school personnel and community-based organizations.

Several studies observe that schools need to develop curricula to address a wider concept of sexual health, including its positive aspects. Materials are needed that break the silence and openly discuss sex and sexuality. Studies found in literature are either NGO based or found in Western contexts. Indian Studies are yet to cover the problem in the context of North East India. Violence against girls has been on the rise in Mizoram, where 40 cases of minor rape had been recorded by the police during the year 2016. Despite the fair sex holding high position in Mizo society, the police figures speak of 21 cases of school girl rape, 72 cases of physical violence and four incidents of domestic violence in 2014. Records reveal cases of sexual harassment and school violence on the rise. Hence, a detailed study with its implications in the context of secondary school system of Mizoram is long overdue found in their conspicuous absence in literature. Further, there is need to study the problem with the help of mixed methods.

Ultimately, the aim is to reduce violence against girls in secondary schools, prepared to cope with today's education system. It is, therefore, necessary to look at the problem of violence and violent behaviour against girls in our schools and suggest a viable mechanism to eradicate of violence and violent behaviour against girls from our schools. In the lights of the above discussion that there is a need to conduct a study in violence against girls and its effect on girls education in secondary schools of Mizoram.

2.8 Research Questions

Keeping the above discussion researcher formulated some research questions which are given below:

1. What are the causes of violence against girls in secondary schools of Mizoram?
2. What are the types of violence against secondary schools of Mizoram?
3. Is there any effect of violence on girl's education?
4. What are the plans and programmes implemented by government of Mizoram to reduce girl's violence in secondary school?
5. What will be the mechanism to reduce violence against girls in secondary school?

2.9 Objective of the study

This project has been incepted with the goal of finding out the situation of girl students with regard to their experience with violence in secondary schools. There to:

1. Identify and classify the causes and the types of violence on girls in and around secondary schools of Mizoram;
2. Assess and establish the effects of violence on girls education in Mizoram;
3. Find out if there are policies and strategies dealing with violence against school girls and assess their effectiveness in tackling the problem;
4. Propose viable mechanisms and holistic ways of addressing the problem by stakeholders at all levels; and
5. Develop a framework for reduction of violence against girls in secondary schools of Mizoram.

3
Methodology

Explanation of the methodology of the study is oriented towards striking out various steps that are generally adopted by a researcher in cracking into the research problem along with the logic behind them. Thus, this chapter explains the broad frame of the research process, the study follows. Methodology of this study speaks why this research study has been undertaken, how the research problem has been identified, what data have been collected and what particular method has been adopted and why particular technique of analyzing data has been used.

The present study has reviewed the related and relevant materials and other pertinent literature for exploring existing knowledge. Survey was conducted on teachers of the schools and other key informants who have had practical experience of the broad problem area and further investigation was done on some specific cases. The specific objectives of the present study decided on the basis of the research gap and the rationale thereof have been discussed in the last section of the previous chapter. Accordingly, this chapter discusses the following heads: the Design of Research, the Selection of the Universe and Sample, Tools Used, Fieldwork Details, Organisational Structure, Methodological Gains and Limitations of the Study. The area of the study and population features is included under the description of Universe and Sample.

3.1 The Design of Research

The formidable problem that follows the task of defining the research problem is the preparation of the design of the research project, popularly known as research design. A research design is the arrangement of conditions for collection and analysis of data in a manner that aims to combine relevance to the research purpose with economy in procedure. This study intends to establish a basis for clarifying concepts establishing priorities for further research and gathering information about practical possibilities for carrying out research in specific real life setting.

The present study has an exploratory-cum-descriptive research design. In this study, the purpose is to formulate a problem for more precise and structured investigation. The research has followed the mixed mode method and has incorporated quantitative and qualitative methodologies to study the nature, nuances and the best practices adopted by the school for mitigating girls violence in secondary school. This way the reader can have a general understanding of the findings by going through the numbers, and a more grounded understanding based on the well triangulated analysis.

3.2 The Selection of the Universe

Universe or population includes all the individuals, belonging to a designated category characterizing specific attributes which a particular study should principally cover. The findings from the sample are applied to the population. Population of this study includes all high school students and stakeholders including the teachers of Mizoram State in North East India.

Northeast India is the eastern-most region of India. It is connected to East India *via* a narrow corridor squeezed between independent nations of Bhutan and Bangladesh. It comprises the contiguous Seven Sister States (Arunachal Pradesh, Assam, Manipur, Meghalaya, Mizoram, Nagaland, and Tripura), and the Himalayan state of Sikkim. Except for the Goalpara region of Assam, the rest did not become part of political India until the 19th century and later. The Brahmaputra valley area of Assam became a part of British India in 1824, with the hill regions annexed later. Sikkim was annexed to the Indian Union

Table 3.1: Population Distribution in Northeast India States (2011 Census)

State	Population	Sex Ratio	Literacy %	Rural Population	Urban Population	Area (km²)	Density (/km²)
Arunachal	13,83,727	938	65.38	8,70,087	2,27,881	83,743	17
Assam	3,12,05,576	958	72.19	2,32,16,288	34,39,240	78,438	397
Manipur	25,70,390	992	79.21	15,90,820	5,75,968	22,327	122
Meghalaya	29,66,889	989	74.43	18,64,711	4,54,111	22,429	132
Mizoram	10,97,206	976	91.33	4,47,567	4,41,006	21,081	52
Nagaland	19,78,502	931	79.55	16,47,249	3,42,787	16,579	119
Sikkim	6,10,577	890	81.42	4,80,981	59,870	7,096	86
Tripura	3,673,917	960	87.22	2,653,453	545,750	10,486	350

Source: Mohanty, R.K., 2016c: 76.

through a referendum in 1975; it was recognized as part of Northeast India in the 1990s.

Northeast India is generally considered one of the most challenging regions of the country to govern. It has been the site of separatist movements among the tribal peoples, Northeast India constitutes about 8 per cent of India's size; roughly three quarters the size of the state of Maharashtra. Its population is approximately 40 million (2011 census), 3.1 per cent of the total Indian population; roughly equal to that of Odisha. Northeast India has over 220 ethnic groups and equal number of dialects. The hills states in the region like Arunachal Pradesh, Meghalaya, Mizoram and Nagaland are predominantly inhabited by tribal people with a degree of diversity even within the tribal groups. The region's population results from ancient and continuous flows of migrations from Tibet, Indo-Gangetic India, the Himalayas, present Bangladesh and Myanmar.

The Siliguri Corridor in West Bengal, with a width of 21 to 40 kilometres (13 to 25 miles), connects the North Eastern region with the main part of India. The region shares more than 4,500 kilometres (2,800 mile) of international border (about 95 per cent of its entire border area) with China (southern Tibet) in the north, Myanmar in the east, Bangladesh in the southwest, and Bhutan to the northwest.

The states are officially recognised under the North Eastern Council (NEC), constituted in 1971 as the acting agency for the development of the eight states. The North Eastern Development Finance Corporation Ltd. (NEDFi) was incorporated on 9 August, 1995 and the Ministry of Development of North Eastern Region (DoNER) was set up in September 2001. A Political Map of North East India is given on page 64 (Fig. 3.1).

Mizoram is one of the seven sisters of Northeast India, bordered by Myanmar (formerly known as Burma) to its east and south, Bangladesh to its west, and the states of Manipur, Assam, and Tripura to its north. Mizoram means 'Land of the Highlanders' and its local language is Mizo. The Mizo Hills, which dominate the state's topography, rise to more than 2000 m (6560 ft) near the Myanmar border. Aizawl, the state capital, is 1220 m (4000 ft) above sea level. The state covers a total area of 8,139.4 sq. miles or 21,087 sq. km. According to the census performed in 2011, the population of the state is 1,091,014.

Mizoram has 8 districts, namely Aizawl, Kolasib, Lawngtlai, Lunglei, Mamit, Siaha, Serchhip, Champhai, with 22 towns and 817 villages. Mizoram comprises a formal system of education which ranges from elementary to university education, training to technical courses. By census 2011, the state has the third highest literacy rate in the country, i.e. 92 per cent. There are about 3900 schools consisting of primary, secondary and senior secondary schools in the state which are either privately owned or are fully or partially managed by the government.

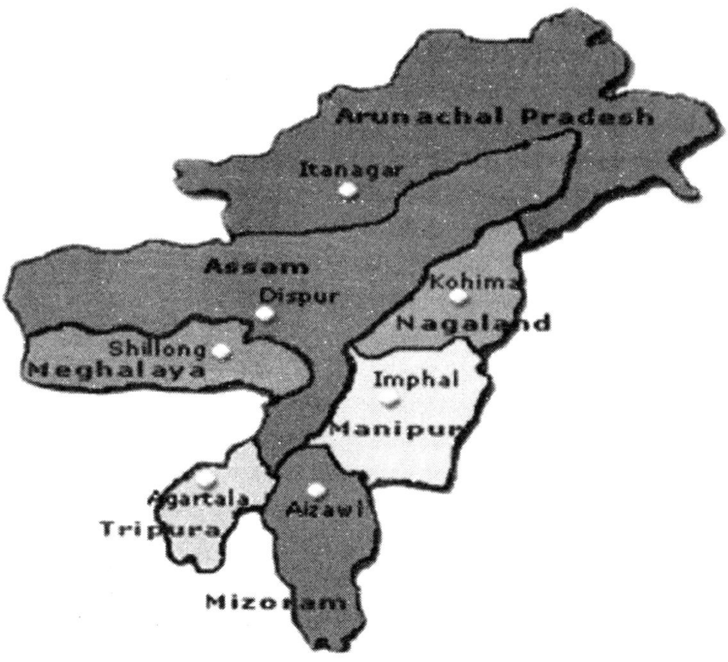

Fig. 3.1: Political Map of North East India

From the above table it is seen that there are 614 secondary schools in Mizoram. The total enrolment in secondary schools is 41534 with 20824 boys and 20710 girls. It seems boy's enrolment ratio is high in comparison to girls. Similarly the number of male teachers is more than number of female teachers working in secondary schools of Mizoram. From this gender dimension of student enrolment and teachers in position can be understood. Inadequacy of lady teachers in schools is directly related to drop out of girls from schools and possibility of violence perpetrated on them.

Table 3.2: Type and Status of Secondary Schools in Mizoram

Sl. No.	Type of schools	No of schools	Total enrolment			No. of teachers		
			Boys	Girls	Total	Male	Female	Total
1	Central Govt.	10	365	313	678	50	25	75
2	State Govt.	199	7773	8153	15926	1014	538	1552
3	RMSA	74	1290	1005	2295	301	201	502
4	Deficit	09	1272	1495	2767	76	55	131
5	Adhoc Aided	129	3834	3896	7730	641	344	985
6	Lump sum aided	27	722	656	1378	108	48	156
7	Private unaided	166	5568	5192	10760	663	330	993
	Total	**614**	**20824**	**20710**	**41534**	**2853**	**1541**	**4394**

Source: Directorate of School Education: Government of Mizoram, 2015-16.

Table 3.3: District-wise Distribution of Secondary Schools in Mizoram

Sl. No.	Name of the district	No of secondary schools	Total enrolment			No of teachers		
			Boys	Girls	Total	Male	Female	Total
1	Aizawl	205	8013	8522	16535	991	607	1598
2	Champhai	85	2382	2524	4906	396	191	587
3	Kolasib	41	1467	1426	2893	198	109	307
4	Lawngtlai	54	2020	1667	3687	230	89	319
5	Lunglei	116	3323	3077	6400	519	275	794
6	Mamit	41	1200	1038	2238	186	90	276
7	Saiha	35	1137	1139	2276	159	75	234
8	Serchhip	37	1282	1317	2599	174	105	279
	Total	**614**	**20824**	**20710**	**41534**	**2853**	**1541**	**4394**

Source: Directorate of School Education: Government of Mizoram, 2015-16.

Table 3.3 clearly indicates the district-wise distribution of secondary schools in Mizoram. The number of secondary schools in Aizawl district is 205 whereas it is very low in Saiha i.e. 35. In Lunglei district it is also 116 and in Kolasib and Mamait district it is 41. The total number of students enrolled in Aizawl district is 16355 with 8013 boys and 8522 girls. In Champhai district the girl enrolment is more than boys whereas in Lawngtalai girls enrolment is less than boys. The same thing is seen in Mamit district also. Following table indicates gross enrolment ratio (GER) at Secondary level in Mizoram.

Table 3.4: Gross Enrolment Ratio (GER) at Secondary Level in Mizoram

Year	Boys	Girls	Total
2014-15	84.65	85.78	85.21
2013-14	86.25	87.19	86.71
2012-13	71.05	69.51	71.16
2011-12	66.97	69.30	68.12
2010-11	64.11	69.11	63.60

Source: U-DISE Data 2015-16, Government of Mizoram.

Although total enrolment of boys is higher against girls in absolute number (Table 3.3), the gross enrolment ratio (GER) of girls at Secondary level show higher rate in Mizoram. A major concern in Mizoram, nay in the country, is to retain the girl's enrolment in schools.

3.3 The Sample

Multistage stratified random sampling procedures were adopted for the study. Initially, when the project was proposed, there were intentions to study secondary schools across 8 districts. The project was later finally sanctioned by Ministry of Women and Child Development, Government of India for 4 districts only (1st Stage). The researcher selected four districts from the north region of Mizoram (2nd Stage), i.e. Aizawl and Champhai (two high incident districts) and Mamit and Kolasib (two low incident districts). In addition, due to Aizawl being the epicentre of the state's commercial, educational and political scenario, it was the first district of choice for the study. The consideration for the selection for the other 3 districts was the distance from Aizawl which would be the base of operations for the Project Director and the project fellows.

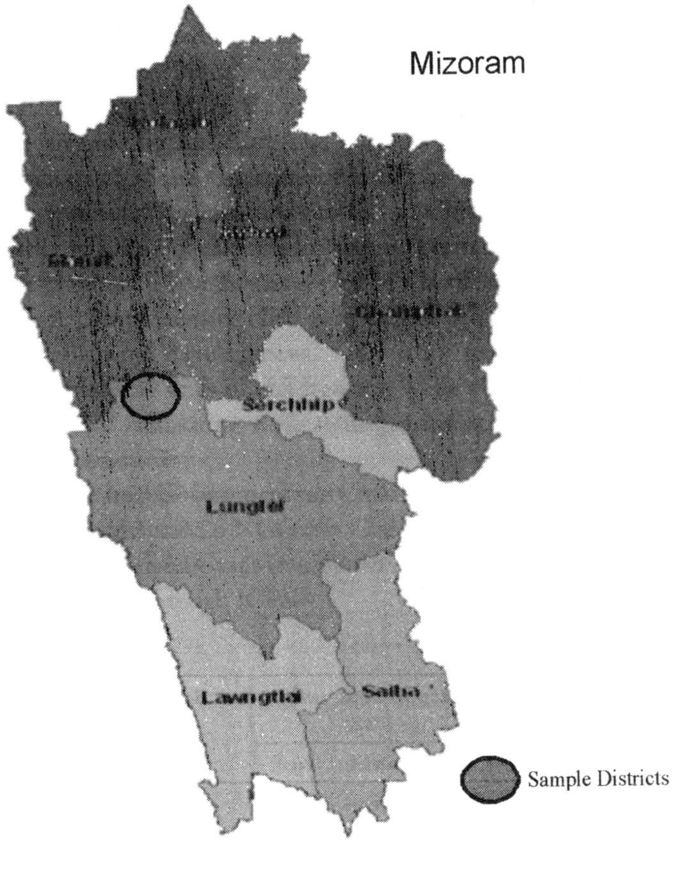

Fig. 3.2: District Map of Mizoram

Then the project director collected the information from the Directorate of School Education, Mizoram. The schools mostly affected by violence and conflicts were identified with the consultation of DEOs of different districts. Then BEOs of the concerned schools were consulted. Then the researcher collected the route chart and other required information about each sample school from the District and Block Headquarters. Ten secondary schools (Government, Non-Government) from each district (5 from rural and 5 from urban) were selected for the study. A total numbering 40 (10 × 4) secondary schools from the entire sample district were selected for the study (3rd Stage).

The investigator met the headmaster from whom he collected different information regarding information about the teachers such as science, arts and PET and students and parents. With the help of headmaster and class teacher from each sample School, the investigator randomly selected 5 students of class IX. 5 girl students from each school, i.e. a number of 200 (40 × 5) were selected for the study (4th Stage). In the same manner, 200 teachers and 200 parents were selected (5 from each school) from same school jurisdictions were also selected for the study (5th Stage).

In addition to secondary school class-IX children, teachers and parents, for holistic analysis respondents also included NGO personnel and government officials. Thus, two NGO personnel and one government official from each district were selected for the present study (6th Stage).

3.4 Account of Population Studied

Table 3.5: Account of Population Studied

Sl. No.	Respondents	Population	Sample taken
1	Districts	8	4
2	Secondary schools	614	40
3	Students (Girls)	20710	200
4	Teachers	4394	200
5	Parents	83068	200
6	NGO's	22	8
7	Government Officials	32	4

Source: Directorate of School Education: Government of Mizoram, 2015-16.

3.5 Sources of Data and Tools Used

Data are all the relevant materials, past and present, serving as bases for study and analysis. They are "the living stuff, with all the relevant emotional signs attached," to one's expressions, actions, attitudes and values within his social world. Data are of two types: Primary and Secondary. The data relating to the research problem collected directly from the respondents using the tools and techniques of data collection are called as primary data and those collected from available literature such as books, journals, magazines, Research reports and Government records are secondary. The researcher has collected both the Primary and Secondary data for giving justice to this piece of research. Here the primary data have been used to bring objectivity to the study and the secondary data have been used to validate the primary data as well as to draw inferences. Tools are the instruments used to collect data and techniques are the skilled ways used in research for the same.

As regards the secondary data, the investigator went through different research reports, journals and magazines on violence against girls in secondary schools written by different authors for the development of the tools. The researcher visited the library of Gandhi Peace Foundation New Delhi, ICSSR, New Delhi and other library having national importance. The Investigator also went through different research reports and Ph.D. thesis prepared on violence against girls and prepared the draft of the interview schedule and questionnaire.

A workshop was organised at Department of Education, Mizoram University for the development of tools, i.e. questionnaire for students, teachers and parents In the said workshop a total 12 professors of Education, Sociology, Psychology and Peace and Conflict Departments of different universities, 5 secondary school teachers, 2 parents and two NGO personnel, three junior project fellow who are working for the project participated. In the said workshop tool was developed for the present study. The following tools have been developed and used to collect data.

1. A questionnaire was developed and used to collect data from the students.
2. A questionnaire was developed and used to collect the views of teachers and parents.
3. An interview schedule was developed to collect data from government official and NGO personnel.

All the drafted questionnaires and schedules were sent to a panel of experts consisting of distinguished educationists and veteran professors, experts working in the field of Education. The purpose was:

- To suggest any other item to be included in the questionnaire and schedules if possible.
- To add any other area of relevance.
- To delete any area or areas, item or items which were not relevant to the present study.
- To correct the ambiguities, biases, poor phrasing and incorrect wording etc.
- To examine the relation between the questionnaire and schedules with objectives of the study.
- It is needless to say that almost all the experts extended their full Co-operation by giving views with valuable suggestions.

After getting their valuable suggestions, necessary correction was made on the drafts. The lists of experts have been given in **Appendix-D.** As both the questionnaires and interview schedule were developed taking the valuable suggestions of these esteemed experts into consideration, these have satisfactory degree of content validity.

After the preparation of final draft of the questionnaire for the students teachers and parents, as per the suggestions and remarks of the experts, the investigator first administered the questionnaire over a sample of 10 students, 10 teachers, and 10 parents from Aizawl district. Each student, teacher, and parent were asked to respond to each item of the questionnaire to give some factual information after getting the responses the investigator tabulated the responses. It was not possible to administer the questionnaire on the entire sample for the reason that the samples were taken from four districts of the state and it was not practicable to cover all the samples again. So to estimate the reliability of the questionnaire the investigator after one month again administered the previous questionnaire on the same sample. The responses taken from the student's teachers and parents in the second time were represented numerically and two sets of scores were obtained for the analysis of responses of students, teachers, and parents.

The investigator, therefore, correlated the two sets of scores by product movement method. The statistical formula used to calculate the coefficient of correlation has been given by Garrett (1971).

$$r_{xy} = \frac{\dfrac{\sum x^1 \ y^1}{N} - C^1 xC^1 \ y}{x^1 y^1}$$

Where x^1, y^1 are the deviations from the assumed mean. N is the size of the sample, C^1s, c^1_y are correlation factors. The detail calculation of coefficient of correlation has given below, and the scattered diagram represented in table.

RELIABILITY

$$Cy = \frac{\sum fy^1}{N} = -\frac{-44}{51} = -0.86 \ Cy^2 = 0.7396$$

$$Cx = \frac{\sum fx^1}{N} = \frac{-44}{51} = -0.86 \ Cx^2 = 0.7396$$

$$\sigma x = \sqrt{\frac{\sum fx^{12}}{N} - cx^2} = \sqrt{\frac{398}{51} - 0.7396} = \sqrt{7.8039 - 0.7396} = \sqrt{7.0643} = 2.6.$$

$$Cy = \frac{\sum x^1 y^1 - Cx - Cy}{\sigma x . \sigma y} = \frac{\dfrac{402}{51} - (-0.860)(-0.86)}{2.83 \times 2.65}$$

$$= \frac{7.88 - 0.7396}{7.4995} = \frac{7.1404}{7.4995}$$

= 0.958 (Highly Significant)

The value of r found 0.958 which is very high. Thus the questionnaire was very reliable.

3.6 Fieldwork

As per the norms of the project 3 fellows were selected from different background of social science, i.e. from Education, Sociology, and Psychology in the month of May 2016, the project fellows also collected the review of literature in the month of May and June 2016. In the month of August 2016 project fellows and project director started their field visit for collection of data.

Then the researcher collected the route chart and other required information about each sample school from the District and Block Head Quarters and started his journeying to each sample school. After reaching the school questionnaire were sent to five parents for collection of data with the help of headmaster of each school.

Then the investigator met the student respondents in their class in the leisure period and established rapport with them. Then the project fellow distributed the questionnaire to the students and requested them to answer the entire question. The investigator explains how to answer the questions. The investigator tried his best to clarify all the doubts of the students. In the same way the investigator selected 5 teachers from each school to collect the perceptions and suggestions of violence against girls in secondary schools. The English version of the questionnaire meant for the students teachers and parents has been given in the Appendix-A.

After the fieldwork, the FGD (Focus Group Discussion) was held in November 2016. Two FGDs were conducted with girls in 2 different senior secondary high schools in Aizawl.

No significant problems arose during the fieldwork. Besides the legwork needed in the snowballing method, contacting the schools and getting permission was a bit time consuming with longer waiting periods at times, mostly due to the problem of scheduling time. A minor encumbrance was the road travel needed to reach the sites due to the general bad condition of highways in the state. These issues are, however, very minor and nothing out of the ordinary in conducting a fieldwork.

3.7 The Schedule of the Project

After the necessary paper work was taken care of, the project took wings in May 2016. The months of June and July were spent gathering literature including reviews. These readings did not only form part of the project write-up but also became an informal guideline for the researchers on how the project was to be envisioned.

In mid-July 2016, as detailed above, a workshop was conducted for the purpose of finalising the structure of the interviews and corresponding schedules. The primary fieldwork was conducted from August to October 2016 in the 4 districts of Aizawl, Kolasib, Mamit and Champhai. The details have been presented above.

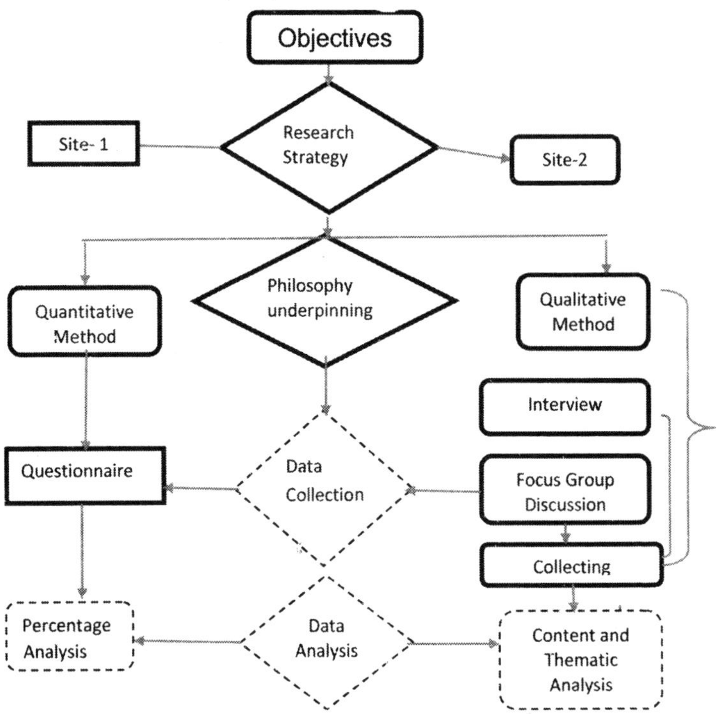

Fig. 3.3: Diagram of Research Process

Source: Analysis by L. Mishra (2016).

November and December of 2016 was spent in the analysis phase with the joint collaboration of all the project fellows under the supervision of the project director. All data was collated and discussions were held along with preliminary write-ups to figure out how the project would look like in its finality. January to March 2017 was dedicated to report writing and finalising the draft of the project. This included editorial changes as well as finalising the conclusion to the project.

Two rounds of dissemination workshop were conducted during first two weeks of April 2017 with the departmental colleagues and research scholars before final printing of the report for submission. Experts from Public Administration, Social Work and Sociology Departments of Mizoram University were invited to the workshops. First round of workshop was devoted towards data dissemination and data cleaning. Second round of workshop was devoted towards finalizing the implication outcome and the authentication of report.

3.8 Organisational Structure

The project had outlined a structure for both the research process and the write up as well. It had determined the objectives to be five-fold:

1. To identify and classify the causes and the types of violence on girls in and around secondary schools of Mizoram.
2. To assess and establish the effects of violence on girls education in Mizoram.
3. To find out if there are policies and strategies dealing with violence against school girls and assess their effectiveness in tackling the problem.
4. To propose viable mechanisms and holistic ways of addressing the problem by stakeholders at all levels.
5. To develop a framework for reduction of violence against girls in secondary schools of Mizoram.

Based on the data collected and the analysis done, the project was then later chapterised in the following manner. In the Introductory Chapter, the issues at hand were contextualized in the form of a general outline, the overall problems to be tackled were highlighted and key concepts were emphasised. Existing literature on the subject was reviewed for the purpose of finding research gaps in Chapter Two.

The third chapter deals mostly with the methodology and tools used for the project, and describes the design and schedule of the project. This chapter also presented an account of the studied population and highlighted the total number of secondary schools in the 4 chosen districts along with its gender dimensions.

The fourth chapter is where all the data unearthed has been presented, along with the analysis. The topic of violence was addressed not only by the adolescent girls, but also by teachers and parents. Furthermore, comparative analysis was made not only on the testimonies across these categories but also across the districts as well. In the end an analysis of the testimonies of key respondents on the topic of the effect of violence on these young girls was made.

The fifth chapter is dealing with the plans and programmes implemented by Government of India and Mizoram for eradicating violence against girls in secondary school.

The final chapter looks back and consolidates the findings in a conclusive manner, and while providing a summary of all that has been done, gives suggestions for what could be done in future research endeavours.

3.9 Methodological Gains

The project utilised the mixed mode method and has in the process reinvigorated the notion that such a method is, as of now in academia, the most wholesome way to pursuing truth. As mentioned before, quantitative and qualitative approaches answer different kinds of questions. Together, they not only provide new knowledge, but also welcome readers to make their own analysis as they have been provided with not only numerical data but also the methodologies involved in the final qualitative analysis.

3.10 Limitations of the Study

Study of girl child in general and more so the offenses against them were quite challenging as they have hitherto been in all their theoretical, methodological and substantive domains. Some difficulties were faced while administering the tools of data collection especially conducting interviews, observation and Focused Group Discussion. The investigator found a general apathy and unwillingness among some respondents to help in conducting interview. They treated with usual suspicion, in case it may expose some of their spontaneous opinions, unfriendly to the organization, the community and authority. But the investigator was making an impression upon them that the study was purely academic in nature and their names will be mentioned nowhere in no circumstances.

For Focused Group Discussion it was very difficult to gather 9-12 respondents at a time for a long period due to their class work and some of them were afraid of group discussion. All these limitations were resolved by convincing the respondents and the school authority on the grounds of the possibility of solution of their problems by sharing the findings with the police organization and the government and the necessity and importance of research on offenses against girl child. Diverting the respondents from their class was difficult as the teachers were committed to their school duty and students did not like to be diverted from the class.

Teachers, NGO officials and government officers were not able to spare sufficient time to discuss, various issues and much more so to come out openly with arguments or counter arguments about the basic issues posed. Further, certain files and correspondences at the school level, which had direct bearing upon the study, were not made available to the scholar on the plea that they were highly confidential. The parents needed continuous pushing and reminders to return the questionnaire.

The literature available on the subject being limited, the researcher had taken all possible care to collect the available ones and the possibility of omissions cannot be denied. While the study has been limited to four districts of the state, nevertheless, its implications can be felt and be applicable to whole of Mizoram.

4
Analysis of Data

Nature of Violence: Victim Perspective and Stakeholder's Perceptions

> "Violence is fomented by the imposition of singular and belligerent identities on gullible people, championed by proficient artisans of terror."—Amartya Sen: *Identity and Violence—The Illusion of Destiny.*

This Chapter relates to description and analysis of data collected from the field. The victim perspective and stakeholder's perceptions of the nature and nuances of violence against girl child in school system in Mizoram have been analysed. First the students were supplied with thirty four types of statements to identify the nature of violence perpetrated against them and the perpetrator of violence. Then students were asked to say if they were ever beaten in the school and if so in what form. The presentation of data on the perception of students regarding the violence perpetrated against them for the purpose of this chapter is operationalized as victim perspective.

4.1 Students' Perceptions about Violence against Girls

Violence is a disturbing issue across the world today. It is a subject of great concern in homes, schools, workplaces, and social places, rural and urban areas. There are many types of school violence, including physical, mental or sexual abuse, theft and vandalism.

Table 4.1: Students' Perceptions on Secondary School Violence against Girls

Sl. No.	Statement	Aizawl			Champhai			Kolasib			Mamit		
		Yes	No	UD	Yes	No	UD	Yes	No	UD	Yes	No	UD
1	Fighting with schoolmates	7 — 14	43 — 86	0 — 0	8 — 16	42 — 84	0 — 0	6 — 12	44 — 88	0 — 0	7 — 14	43 — 86	0 — 0
2	Stealing	4 — 8	46 — 92	0 — 0	5 — 10	42 — 84	3 — 6	10 — 20	39 — 78	1 — 2	4 — 8	46 — 92	0 — 0
3	Seizing food	8 — 16	42 — 84	0 — 0	2 — 4	48 — 96	0 — 0	7 — 14	43 — 86	0 — 0	6 — 12	44 — 88	0 — 0
4	Intentional stepping or pushing	7 — 14	43 — 86	0 — 0	12 — 24	38 — 76	0 — 0	20 — 40	27 — 54	3 — 6	2 — 4	48 — 96	0 — 0
5	Pulling ear by teachers	3 — 6	47 — 94	0 — 0	15 — 30	35 — 70	0 — 0	20 — 40	30 — 60	0 — 0	14 — 28	36 — 72	0 — 0
6	Force dating by students	11 — 22	39 — 78	0 — 0	0 — 0	50 — 100	0 — 0	1 — 2	48 — 96	1 — 2	6 — 12	43 — 86	1 — 2

(Contd.)

Sl. No.	Statement	Aizawl			Champhai			Kolasib			Mamit		
		Yes	No	UD	Yes	No	UD	Yes	No	UD	Yes	No	UD
7	Force kissing by students	4 — 8	46 — 92	0 — 0	1 — 2	49 — 98	0 — 0	2 — 4	46 — 92	2 — 4	0 — 0	50 — 100	0 — 0
8	Sexual gestures by students	2 — 4	48 — 96	0 — 0	4 — 8	35 — 70	1 — 2	2 — 4	43 — 86	5 — 10	1 — 2	49 — 98	0 — 0
9	Touching restricted body part by student	8 — 16	40 — 80	2 — 4	4 — 8	36 — 72	0 — 0	7 — 14	41 — 82	2 — 4	0 — 0	50 — 100	0 — 0
10	Trying for sex by school boy	0 — 0	49 — 98	1 — 2	0 — 0	50 — 100	0 — 0	0 — 0	48 — 96	2 — 4	0 — 0	50 — 100	0 — 0
11	Disturbing message, letters	8 — 16	42 — 84	0 — 0	1 — 2	49 — 98	0 — 0	4 — 8	43 — 86	3 — 6	0 — 0	50 — 100	0 — 0
12	Touching restricted body part by teacher	5 — 10	45 — 90	0 — 0	1 — 2	49 — 98	0 — 0	0 — 0	43 — 86	5 — 10	4 — 8	46 — 92	0 — 0

(Contd.)

Sl. No.	Statement	Aizawl			Champhai			Kolasib			Mamit		
		Yes	No	UD	Yes	No	UD	Yes	No	UD	Yes	No	UD
13	Showing unhealthy pictures	4/8	45/90	1/2	0/0	50/100	0/0	0/0	48/96	2/4	6/12	44/88	0/0
14	Force kissing by teacher	0/0	50/100	0/0	0/0	50/100	0/0	0/0	48/96	2/4	0/0	50/100	0/0
15	Trying for sex by teacher	0/0	50/100	0/0	0/0	50/100	0/0	0/0	48/96	2/4	3/6	47/94	0/0
16	Threatening for refusing sex	3/6	47/94	0/0	0/0	50/100	0/0	0/0	47/94	3/6	8/16	42/84	0/0
17	Rejecting by peers	0/0	50/100	0/0	9/18	40/80	1/2	9/18	41/82	0/0	9/18	41/82	0/0
18	Rejecting by teacher	0/0	50/100	0/0	1/2	48/96	1/2	3/6	47/94	0/0	4/8	46/92	0/0

(Contd.)

Sl. No.	Statement	Aizawl			Champhai			Kolasib			Mamit		
		Yes	No	UD	Yes	No	UD	Yes	No	UD	Yes	No	UD
19	Humiliating	0 — 0	50 — 50	0 — 0	11 — 12	36 — 72	3 — 6	17 — 34	32 — 64	1 — 2	2 — 4	48 — 96	0 — 0
20	Rejecting request for menstruation	0 — 0	49 — 98	1 — 2	4 — 8	41 — 82	50 — 100	4 — 8	46 — 92	0 — 0	3 — 6	47 — 94	0 — 0
21	Teasing for monthly period	1 — 2	47 — 94	2 — 4	3 — 6	43 — 86	4 — 8	1 — 2	49 — 98	0 — 0	0 — 0	50 — 100	0 — 0
22	Neglecting by teachers	0 — 0	48 — 96	2 — 4	1 — 2	48 — 96	1 — 2	3 — 6	45 — 90	2 — 4	0 — 0	49 — 98	1 — 2
23	Assaulted by schoolmates	8 — 16	42 — 84	0 — 0	14 — 28	36 — 72	0 — 0	19 — 38	31 — 62	0 — 0	0 — 0	50 — 100	0 — 0
24	Using bad, abusive language	7 — 14	43 — 86	0 — 0	3 — 6	47 — 94	0 — 0	18 — 36	31 — 62	1 — 2	0 — 0	50 — 100	0 — 0

(*Contd.*)

Sl. No.	Statement	Aizawl			Champhai			Kolasib			Mamit		
		Yes	No	UD	Yes	No	UD	Yes	No	UD	Yes	No	UD
25	Scolding ruthlessly	3/6	47/94	0/0	5/10	44/88	1/2	18/36	32/64	0/0	0/0	50/100	0/0
26	Assaulted by teachers	1/2	49/98	0/0	4/8	46/92	0/0	8/16	41/82	1/2	0/0	50/100	0/0
27	Beating by teachers	2/4	48/96	0/0	1/2	47/94	2/4	4/8	46/92	0/0	6/12	43/86	1/2
28	Slapping by teachers	0/0	49/98	1/0	2/4	48/96	0/0	0/0	50/100	0/0	0/0	49/98	1/2
29	Bullying orally by teachers	4/8	40/80	6/12	7/14	39/78	4/8	9/18	30/60	11/22	6/12	42/84	2/4
30	Molesting by students	7/14	30/60	13/26	9/18	40/80	1/2	6/12	41/82	3/6	3/6	35/70	10/20

(*Contd.*)

Sl. No.	Statement	Aizawl			Champhai			Kolasib			Mamit		
		Yes	No	UD	Yes	No	UD	Yes	No	UD	Yes	No	UD
31	Molesting by teachers	1/2	49/98	0/0	0/0	50/100	0/0	2/4	47/94	1/2	0/0	47/94	3/6
32	Asking for date by teachers	1/2	48/96	1/2	0/0	49/98	1/2	0/0	48/96	2/4	0/0	46/92	4/8
33	Asking sex for marks by teachers	0/0	50/100	0/0	0/0	50/100	0/0	0/0	49/98	1/2	0/0	50/0	0/0
34	Experience attempt of Rape	0/0	50/100	0/0	0/0	50/100	0/0	50/100	0/0	50/100	0/0	50/100	0/0

Note: The figure in the numerators indicate the percentage and that of the denominators indicate the corresponding number.

Schools cannot ignore the need to create a safe environment by coordinating deterrents to violence through discipline, prevention, and education. Because schools alone cannot eliminate the problem of violence, students must also be involved by working with the schools to create a safe and nurturing environment which fosters learning. The study includes a section in which perceptions of secondary school girls on violence are described.

From Table 4.1, it is found that in Aizawl District, only 7 students, i.e. 14% have experienced fighting with their classmates and the rest 86% did not experience such things. 4 girls, i.e. 8% reported their belongings had been stolen by other students and 92% did not experience so. 42 students, i.e. 84% did not experience anyone in their school seizing their food while 8 students, i.e. 16% agreed they experienced someone seizing their food. 14% of the girls agreed that there are some schoolmates who intentionally step on them and push them; the rest 86% did not experience such things. 3 girls, i.e. 6% agreed their teachers used to punish them by pulling their ear. 11 girls, i.e. 22% reported that the boys from their school try to take them on a date forcefully. There were 4 girls, i.e. 8% who reported that the boys from their school tried to kiss them by force and there were also 2 girls who reported that the male students made sexual gestures towards them. 8 girls, i.e. 16% of the girls agreed that their schoolmates touched restricted parts of their body by force. None reported boys trying to have sex with them. 8 girls reported that they received disturbing messages relating to sexual abuse.

Four girls reported teachers showing unhealthy pictures, but none of them faced attempted sex. But 3 girls reported teachers threatening for refusing sex. No one felt rejected among peers or by teachers, and none were humiliated by their teachers when they gave wrong answers. None reported the teacher rejecting their request to leave the class/ school when having menstruation issues and only one was teased. 16% of the girls accepted that their schoolmates tried to assault them by making remarks on their physical appearance and 2% of the girls accepted that their teachers also tried to assault them. There were 10 girls, i.e. 20% who reported that their teachers used bad and abusive language against them, or were scolded ruthlessly by their teachers in front of others.

In Champhai district, only 8 students, i.e. 16% have experienced fighting with their classmates and the rest 84% did not experience such things. 5 girls, i.e. 10% reported their properties had been stolen by other students, another 84% did not experience so, and 6% was undecided. Almost all the students, i.e. 96% did not experience anyone in their school seizing their food while 2 students, i.e. 4% agreed they experienced someone seizing their food. 24% of the girls agreed that there are some schoolmates who intentionally step on them and push them, the rest 76% did not experience such things. 15 girls, i.e. 30% agreed their teachers used to punish them by pulling their ear. All the girls reported that the boys from their school never try to take them on a date forcefully. There is one girl, i.e. 2% who reported that the boys from her school tried to kiss her by force, and there were 4 girls who reported that the male students made sexual gestures towards them. 4 girls, i.e. 8% of the girls agreed that their schoolmates touched restricted parts of their body by force. None reported boys trying to have sex with them. Only one girl agreed that she used to receive disturbing messages relating to sexual abuse. No students reported that the teachers made sexual gestures towards them or asked them for a date. There is one girl who agreed that the teacher touched restricted parts of her body. No one reported teachers showing unhealthy pictures, the teacher trying to have sex with them, and the teacher threatening for refusing sex. There were 9 girls, i.e. 18% who felt rejected among peers, and there is one girl who agreed that the teachers were rejecting her. 22% of the girls have remarked that they were humiliated by their teachers when they gave wrong answers. 4 girls reported the teacher rejecting their request to leave the class/school when having menstruation issues. And 3 girls have agreed the teachers used to tease them when seeking permission to leave the class due to monthly period. 28% of the girls accepted that their schoolmates tried to assault them by making remarks on their physical appearance and 8% of the girls accepted that their teachers also tried to assault them. There were 3 girls, i.e. 6% who reported that their teachers used bad and abusive language against them, and 5 girls accepted that they were scolded ruthlessly by their teachers in front of others.

In Kolasib District, out of the 50 students, 6 students i.e.12% agreed that they had been in a fight with their schoolmates and 44 students, i.e. 88% answered no and 0 students, i.e. 0% was undecided. 10 students i.e. 20% answered yes to stealing the belongings of their schoolmates, 39 students, i.e. 78% answered no with the statement and 1 student, i.e. 2% were undecided. There were 7 students, i.e. 14% who admitted to seizing food and 43 students, i.e. 86% answered no and 0 students, i.e. 0% was undecided. There were 20 students, i.e. 40% who have answered yes to have been intentionally pushed or step on by their schoolmates and 27 students, i.e. 54% answered no and 3 students, i.e. 6% were undecided. There were 20 students, i.e. 40% who have been pulled in the ear by the teacher, 30 students, i.e. 60% answered no and 0 students, i.e. 0% was undecided. There was 1 student who was forced to go on a date by classmates, i.e. 2%, 48 students who answered no, i.e. 98% and 1 student, i.e. 2% were undecided. There were 2 students, i.e. 4% who have been forcefully kissed by their classmates, 46 students, i.e. 92% answered no and 2 students, i.e. 4% were undecided. 2 students, i.e. 4% have been sexual harassed, 43, i.e. 86 % of the students answered no and 5 students, i.e. 10% was undecided. There were 7 students, i.e. 14% who have been touched in restricted parts by their schoolmates and 41, i.e. 82% answered no and 2, i.e. 4% of them were undecided. 4 students, i.e. 8% have received disturbing messages and pictures by classmates, 43, i.e. 86% of the students answered no and 3 students, i.e. 6% were undecided. There were 0 students, i.e. 0% who had been touched inappropriately by their teachers, 43, i.e. 86% answered no and 5, i.e. 10% of the students were undecided. There were 0 students, i.e. 0% who have received disturbing messages and pictures from their teachers, 48, i.e. 96% of them answered no to the statement and 2, i.e. 4% of the students were undecided. There were 0, i.e. 0% of students who have been forcefully kissed by their teachers and, 48, i.e. 96% who answered no and 2, i.e. 4% of them were undecided. There were 0, i.e. 0% students who have been asked for sex by their teachers, 48 i.e., 96% answered no and 2, i.e. 4% of them were undecided. 0 students, i.e. 0% who have been threatened for refusing sex by their teachers and 47 students, i.e. 94% answered no and 3 students, i.e. 6% were undecided. There were 9 students i.e.18% who feel being rejected by their peers, 41 students, i.e. 82% answered no with the statement and 0 students, i.e. 0% was undecided. There were 3 students, i.e. 6% who feel rejected by their teachers, 47 students, i.e. 94% answered no and 0 students, i.e. 0% was undecided. There were 17 students, i.e. 34% who have been humiliated in front of teachers by their teachers, and 32 students, i.e. 64% answered no and 1 student, i.e. 2% were undecided. There were 4 students, i.e. 8% who have been rejected to leave the class during menstruation period by their teachers, 46 students, i.e. 92% answered no and 0 students, i.e. 0% was undecided. There is 1 student who has been teased for monthly period by the teacher, i.e. 2%, 49 students who answered no, i.e. 98% and 0 students, i.e. 0% was undecided. There were 3 students, i.e. 6% who feel neglected by teachers, 45 students, i.e. 90% answered no and 2 students, i.e. 4% were undecided. 19 students, i.e. 38% have been assaulted by their schoolmates, 31, i.e. 62% of the students answered no and 0 students, i.e. 0% was undecided. There were 18 students, i.e. 36% who have been verbally abused and 31, i.e. 62% answered no and 1, i.e. 2% of them was undecided. There were 18 students, i.e. 36% who have been scolded ruthlessly by the teacher, 32, i.e. 64% who answered no and 0, i.e. 0% the student was undecided. 8 students, i.e. 16% have been assaulted by the teacher, 41, i.e. 82% of the students answered no and 1 student, i.e. 2% was undecided. There were 4 students, i.e. 8% who have been beaten by the teacher, 46, i.e. 92% answered no. There were 50, i.e. 100% of them answered no to the statement. There were 9, i.e. 18% of students who have been verbally abused by the teachers and, 30, i.e. 60% answered no and 11, i.e. 22% of them were undecided. There were 6, i.e. 12% students who had been molested by their schoolmates, 41, i.e. 82% answered no and 3, i.e. 6% of them were undecided. There were 2, i.e. 4% of students who have been molested by their teachers, 47, i.e. 94% answered no and one, i.e. 2% was undecided. There were 0, i.e. 0% of student who has been asked on a date by teachers, who answered no and 2 i.e.4% of students who were undecided. There were 48 i.e.96% student who have been asked for sex to increase their marks, 49, i.e. 98% answered no and one, i.e. 2% was undecided. There were 0, i.e. 0% who has experienced an attempt of rape.

In Mamit District, only 14% of the girls have experienced fighting with their schoolmates and the rest 86% did not experience it. 46 girls, i.e. 92% showed that they did not experience anyone stealing their belongings while 8% agreed some of their properties had been stolen by other students. 88% did not experience others seizing their food while 12% experienced it so. 4% of the girls agreed that there are some schoolmates who intentionally stepped on them or pushed them while 96% remarked that these things did not happen to them. Majority of the respondents, i.e. 72% accepted that their teachers punished them by pulling their ear.

There were 12% of the girls who accepted that there were times that the boys try to take them on a date forcefully but none were kissed by force. 98% of the girls were assured that none of the male students make sexual gestures towards them. None reported of schoolmates touching restricted parts of their body by force or of boys trying to have sex with them, and none received disturbing messages or letters relating to sexual abuse. 8% agreed that there were teachers who touched restricted parts of their body while 92% did not agree to this statement. None reported teachers while 4% were left undecided. 12% reported teachers ever showing them any kind of unhealthy pictures while 88% did not face this.

None faced schoolmates trying to assault them by making persistent remarks on their physical appearance and body size, no one said that the teachers used bad and abusive language against them, no one was ruthlessly scolded by teachers in front of classmates, and no one was assaulted by teachers through persistent remarks on their physical appearance.

Eighteen percentage of the girls felt that they were rejected among their peers but no one was rejected by the teachers or felt neglected by them. There were only 6% who reported that their teacher rejected their request to leave the classroom when they have menstruation period, and the rest 94% did not agree. None of the girls reported their teachers teasing them when they sought permission to leave the class due to their monthly period.

4.2 Different Kinds of Violence against Girls in Secondary Schools

Perpetrators of violence in secondary schools not only include the classmates, family members, street hooligans but also the teachers in the schools as could be seen in the foregoing paragraphs. Here below an attempt is made to see if the teachers were beating the students in

Table 4.2: The Instruments Used by Teachers to Beat the Respondents and their Peers

Sl. No.	Statement	Aizawl			Champhai			Kolasib			Mamit		
		Yes	No	UD	Yes	No	UD	Yes	No	UD	Yes	No	UD
1	**Did any of your teachers beat you?**	10 — 20	40 — 80	0 — 0	12 — 24	37 — 74	1 — 2	37 — 74	13 — 26	0 — 0	32 — 64	18 — 36	0 — 0
	(a) Cane	0 — 0	50 — 100	0 — 0	0 — 0	50 — 100	0 — 0	0 — 0	50 — 100	0 — 0	0 — 0	50 — 100	0 — 0
	(b) Duster	0 — 0	50 — 100	0 — 0	0 — 0	50 — 100	0 — 0	2 — 4	48 — 96	0 — 0	1 — 2	49 — 98	0 — 0
	(c) Stick	10 — 20	40 — 80	0 — 0	11 — 22	39 — 78	0 — 0	33 — 66	17 — 34	0 — 0	30 — 60	20 — 40	0 — 0
	(d) Belt	0 — 0	50 — 100	0 — 0	0 — 0	50 — 100	0 — 0	0 — 0	50 — 100	0 — 0	0 — 0	50 — 100	0 — 0
	(e) Hands	0 — 0	50 — 100	0 — 0	1 — 2	49 — 98	0 — 0	2 — 4	48 — 96	0 — 0	1 — 2	49 — 98	0 — 0

(*Contd.*)

Sl. No.	Statement	Aizawl			Champhai			Kolasib			Mamit		
		Yes	No	UD	Yes	No	UD	Yes	No	UD	Yes	No	UD
2	**Did any of your teachers beat any of the girls?**	15/30	33/66	2/4	14/28	35/70	1/2	39/78	11/22	0/0	40/80	10/20	0/0
	(a) Cane	0/0	50/100	0/0	0/0	50/100	0/0	2/4	48/96	0/0	1/2	49/98	0/0
	(b) Duster	0/0	50/100	0/0	0/0	50/100	0/	1/2	49/98	0/0	0/0	50/100	0/0
	(c) Stick	15/30	33/66	2/4	14/28	35/70	1/2	38/76	12/24	0/0	38/76	12/24	0/0
	(d) Belt	0/0	50/100	0/0	0/0	50/100	0/0	0/0	50/100	0/0	0/0	50/100	0/0
	(e) Hands	2/4	48/92	0/0	1/2	49/98	0/0	2/4	48/96	0/0	1/2	49/98	0/0

Note: The figure in the numerator indicate the percentage and that of the denominators indicate the corresponding number.

the school. The following table indicates the means/instruments that the teachers used to beat the respondents and their peers.

From Table 4.8 it is found that, in Aizawl District, out of 50 students, 10 girls, i.e. 20% agreed that they were beaten by their teachers with stick. No one was beaten in any other form. 30% reported that they witnessed teachers beating other girls in school, and 15 girls have seen their teachers beating their friends with sticks and 2 girls have witnessed the teacher slapping other girls. In Champhai District, out of 50 students, 12 girls, i.e. 24% agreed that they were beaten by their teachers with sticks. There is only one student who reported being slapped by the teacher. Fourteen, i.e. 28% reported that they witnessed teachers beating other girls in school, and they have seen their teachers beating their friends with sticks and one girl witnessed the teachers slapping other girls.

In Kolasib district, it is found that 37 girls, i.e. 74% were beaten up by their teachers, and among them 70% agreed that they were beaten up with a stick, while only 4% specified they were slapped. Majority, i.e. 78% have witnessed teachers beating other girls, and it can be seen that 76% of the girls were beaten with stick.

In Mamit District, it is found that 32 girls, i.e. 64% of the students were beaten up by their teachers, and among them 70% agreed that they were beaten up with a stick, while only 1 girl was slapped. Majority, i.e. 80% have witnessed teachers beating other girls, and it can be seen that 76% of the girls were mostly beaten up by stick.

From the above analysis it is seen that most of the teachers punish the students largely using sticks and sometimes by using hands through slapping as against any other means listed in the table. Further such incidence is found to be very high in Kolasib and Champai as against that in Aizawl and Mamit Districts.

Comparison Among the Four Districts

Fighting with classmate is relatively higher in Champhai district whereas Kolasib district has higher percentage of stealing the belongings by classmates as against other three districts. Snatching and seizing of food items by friends is found in the urban Aizawl as against the other periphery districts. Internal assault by stepping on the feet and pushing is highest in Kolasib district. Twisting of ear by teachers is highest in Kolasib district though relatively meagre in Aizawl district. This may leave the impression that near the headquarters lesser is the abuse of girl students by the teachers. However, to the contrary, sexual attempts by the teachers by touching the restricted parts of the girls, assaults, asking for date by teachers are highest in Aizawl district. Whereas bullying orally by teachers is highest in Mamit district. Trying for sex as exclusively response from students by the teachers is not found in any other district except Kolasib. Dating and kissing by force, sending messages and disturbing letters by friends, chatting with whatsapp and facebook are more in Aizawl district. Molestation attempt by classmates are highest in Champhai district. Beating by teachers is highest in Kolasib district and slapping by teachers is only found in Champhai district. On the whole, policy issues and their implementations in connection with violence against girls in secondary schools are more at stake at Aizawl than other districts under investigation.

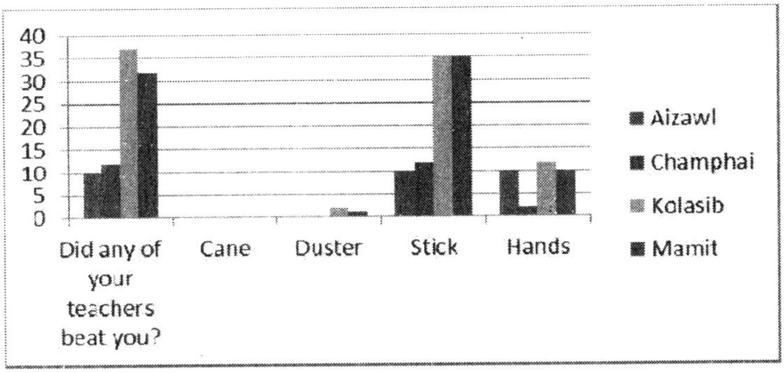

Fig. 4.1: Graphical representation kinds of beating to students

Box-1

During Personal Interview one of the students in Kolasib narrated her experience of being beaten by the teachers. She said, "Out of all the teachers, I am most afraid of my mathematics teacher since class IX. I am very weak in mathematics; therefore, I always copy the notes from my classmates and submit the same along with the others. One day I was waiting for my friend to arrived at school so that I could copy from her, but she did not come to school that day. The teacher on his arrival in the classroom collected our notebook and found

(*Contd.*)

that the no. of copies to be 29 as against 30. The class representative of my class told him that I have not submitted my homework. The teacher became furious and started beating me. I was trembling in fear, I was afraid not of being beaten by my teacher but of the message going to my parents, because when my parents found out they would give me more beating. Since then though poor in mathematics I take care that my math homework is done and submitted to the teachers for correction.

Fig. 4.2: Personal Interview in Kolasib

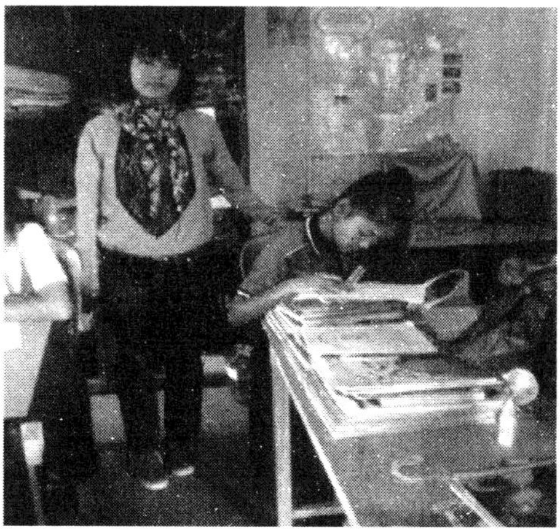

Fig. 4.3: Guided Interview in Chhampai

Box-2

I do not like the teacher calling us to meet them alone in the pretext of correcting answer script and taking the opportunity to touch my restricted parts. This is highly discouraging and dangerous.

Box-3

One day I complain against a teacher of my class to my Miss. She advised me to forget, forgive and ignore. Such incident sometimes hurt me. Especially, as my Madam is not realizing my problems and concerns. I cannot have respect for such teachers.

Fig. 4.4: Personal interview in Mamit district

Box-4

During an interview, one student confesses about how she was bullied at school. She said, "I was bullied a lot at school because of my family background. Not everyone was bullying me but some girls from my class were looking down on me and would often take my things or tear my notebook and they would intentionally try to get me in trouble. After a long period of time I finally have the courage to report it to my teacher who helped me with my problems."

Fig. 4.5: Group discussion in Aizawl District

Box-5

One of my senior from school used to have a crush on me. One day he confesses but since I was not interested I decline his offer. He became furious and would start sending me messages all the time, threatening me and sending me vulgar messages. At first I did not take it seriously but then as he did not stop I became worried. He would even spread false rumor about me to destroy my reputation. I decided to block all his number and avoid him as much as I can so that he would not have any means to contact me or harass me ever again.

4.3 Perceptions of Teachers on Violence against Girls

Teachers are often the staffs that seem to be directly involved in violent actions. Student participants reported that when they faced with violent behaviours, their teachers warned, threatened, and employed corporal punishment to deal with perpetrators.From the table it is found that in Aizawl District, out of the 50 teachers, 29 teachers, i.e. 58% agreed that poor supervision of the school authorities has led to violence against girls in school, 17 teachers, i.e. 34% did not agree and 4 teachers, i.e. 8% were undecided. 19 teachers, i.e. 38% agreed that peer group influence acts as the common cause of violence amongst the students; 24 teachers, i.e. 38% disagreed with the statement and 7 teachers, i.e. 14% were undecided

There were 20 teachers, i.e. 40% who agreed that excessive use of mobile phones plays a role; 29 teachers, i.e. 58% disagreed with the statement and 1 teacher, i.e. 2% was undecided. 21 teachers, i.e. 42% agreed that the lack of discipline in the school is one of the reasons of violence against girls, and 21 teachers, i.e. 42% disagreed and 8 teachers, i.e. 16% are undecided. There are 22 teachers who blamed domestic conflict as one of the causes, 13 teachers, i.e. 26% disagreed and 15 teachers, i.e. 30% are undecided. 36 teachers, i.e. 72% agreed that violent behaviour exhibited by parents has a great influence in inducing violence, 7 teachers, i.e. 14% disagreed and 7 teachers, i.e. 14% are undecided. There are 22 teachers, i.e. 44% who blamed adolescence period, 10 teachers, i.e. 20% disagreed and 18, i.e. 36% of the teachers are undecided. 16 teachers, i.e. 32% agreed that imitation from mass media is one of the causing factors, 19, i.e. 38% of the teachers disagreed with the statement and 15, i.e. 30% of the teachers were undecided. There were 12, i.e. 24% of teachers who agreed that the lack of recreational opportunities and facilities amounted to a moderately high degree of violence and 20, i.e. 40% of the teachers disagreed and 18, i.e. 36% of them are undecided. There are 19 teachers i.e.38% who agreed that absence of teachers causes violence, 23, i.e. 46% of the teachers disagreed with the statement and 8, i.e. 16% of the teachers are undecided. 32, i.e. 64% of the teachers agreed that lack of guidance and counselling leads to violence, 12, i.e. 24% of the teachers disagreed and 6 teachers, i.e. 12% were undecided.

Table 4.3: Perceptions of Teachers on Violence against Secondary School Girls

Sl. No.	Statement	Aizawl			Champhai			Mamit			Kolasib		
		Yes	No	UD	Yes	No	UD	Yes	No	UD	Yes	No	UD
1	Poor supervision by school authorities	29 — 58	17 — 34	4 — 8	20 — 40	29 — 58	1 — 2	29 — 58	17 — 34	4 — 8	20 — 40	18 — 36	12 — 24
2	Peer group influence	19 — 38	24 — 48	7 — 14	35 — 70	11 — 22	4 — 8	35 — 70	8 — 16	7 — 14	28 — 56	16 — 32	6 — 12
3	Excessive use of mobile phones	20 — 40	29 — 58	1 — 2	35 — 70	12 — 24	3 — 6	34 — 68	5 — 10	11 — 22	34 — 68	9 — 18	7 — 14
4	Lack of discipline in School	21 — 42	21 — 42	8 — 16	33 — 66	17 — 34	0 — 0	25 — 50	15 — 30	10 — 20	24 — 48	19 — 38	7 — 14
5	Domestic conflict	22 — 44	13 — 26	15 — 30	40 — 80	8 — 16	2 — 4	36 — 72	6 — 12	8 — 16	30 — 60	7 — 14	13 — 36
6	Violent behaviour exhibited by parents	36 — 72	7 — 14	7 — 14	43 — 86	5 — 10	2 — 4	43 — 86	1 — 2	6 — 12	44 — 88	2 — 4	4 — 8

(Contd.)

Sl. No.	Statement	Aizawl			Champhai			Mamit			Kolasib		
		Yes	No	UD	Yes	No	UD	Yes	No	UD	Yes	No	UD
7	Adolescence period	22 — 44	10 — 20	18 — 36	30 — 60	14 — 28	6 — 12	37 — 74	3 — 6	10 — 20	25 — 50	15 — 30	10 — 20
8	Imitation from mass media	16 — 32	19 — 38	15 — 30	43 — 86	6 — 12	1 — 2	39 — 78	7 — 14	4 — 8	43 - 86	3 — 6	4 — 8
9	Lack of recreation	12 — 24	20 — 40	18 — 36	27 — 54	19 — 38	4 — 8	31 — 62	8 — 16	11 — 22	21 — 42	18 — 36	11 — 22
10	Absence of teachers	19 — 38	23 — 46	8 — 16	31 — 62	18 — 36	1 — 2	34 — 68	12 — 24	4 — 8	24 — 48	21 — 42	5 — 10
11	Lack of guidance and counselling	32 — 64	12 — 24	6 — 12	40 — 80	8 — 16	2 — 4	45 — 90	4 — 8	1 — 2	45 — 90	4 — 8	1 — 2
12	Tuition given by teachers	6 — 12	29 — 58	15 — 30	21 — 42	25 — 50	4 — 8	9 — 18	31 — 62	10 — 20	12 — 24	32 — 64	6 — 12

(*Contd.*)

Sl. No.	Statement	Aizawl			Champhai			Mamit			Kolasib		
		Yes	No	UD	Yes	No	UD	Yes	No	UD	Yes	No	UD
13	Partiality, prejudices, injustice by elder people	26/52	12/24	12/24	36/72	10/20	4/8	35/70	2/4	13/26	31/62	7/14	12/24
14	Uncongenial school environment	28/56	10/20	12/24	37/74	8/16	5/10	27/54	8/16	15/30	28/56	13/26	9/18
15	Lack of interest in school	18/36	25/50	7/14	28/56	19/38	3/6	27/54	13/26	10/20	29 --58	12/24	9/18

Note: The figure in the numerator indicate the percentage and that of the denominators indicate the corresponding number.

There were 6 teachers, i.e. 12% who agreed that tuition given by the teachers leads to different types of violence, 29, i.e. 58% disagreed and 15, i.e. 30% of the teachers were undecided. There were 26 i.e.52% of the teachers who blamed partiality, prejudices and injustice done to the child by the parents, elders and teachers, 12, i.e. 24% of them disagreed with the statement and 12, i.e. 24% of the teachers are undecided. 28, i.e. 56% of the teachers agreed violence occurs more in uncongenial school environment, 10, i.e. 20% of the teachers disagreed and 12, i.e. 24% of them were undecided. 18, i.e. 36% of the teachers blamed lack of interest in school, 25, i.e. 50% disagreed and 7, i.e. 14% of the teachers were undecided.

In Mamit district, out of the 50 teachers, 29 teachers, i.e. 58% agreed poor supervision of the school authorities has led to violence against girls in school and 17 teachers, i.e. 34% did not agree and 4 teachers, i.e. 8% were undecided. 35 teachers i.e. 70% agreed that peer group influence acts as the common cause on violence amongst girls, 8 teachers, i.e. 16% disagreed with the statement and 7 teachers, i.e. 14% were undecided. There were 34 teachers, i.e. 68% who agreed that excessive use of mobile phones plays a role and 5 teachers, i.e. 10% disagreed with the statement and 11 teachers, i.e. 22% are undecided. 25 teachers, i.e. 30% agreed that the lack of discipline in the school is one of the reasons of violence against girls, and 15 teachers, i.e. 30% disagreed and 10 teachers, i.e. 20% were undecided. There were 36 teachers, i.e. 72% who blamed domestic conflict as one of the causes, 6 teachers, i.e. 12% disagreed and 8 teachers, i.e. 16% were undecided. 43 teachers, i.e. 86% agreed that violent behaviour exhibited by parents has a great influence in inducing violence, 1 teacher, i.e. 2% disagreed and 6 teachers, i.e. 12% are undecided. There are 37 teachers, i.e. 74% who blamed adolescence period, 3 teachers, i.e. 6% disagreed and 10, i.e. 20% of the teachers were undecided. 39 teachers, i.e. 78% agreed that imitation from mass media is one of the causing factor, 7, i.e. 14% of the teachers disagreed with the statement and 4, i.e. 8% of the teachers were undecided. There were 31, i.e. 62% of teachers who agreed that the lack of recreational opportunities and facilities amounted to a moderately high degree of violence and 8, i.e. 16% of the teachers disagreed and 11, i.e. 22% of them were undecided. There were 34 teachers, i.e. 68% who agreed that absence of teachers causes violence, 12, i.e. 24% of the teachers disagreed with the statement and 4, i.e. 8% of the teachers were undecided. 45, i.e. 90% of the teachers agreed that lack of guidance and counselling leads to violence, 4, i.e. 8% of the teachers disagreed and 1 teacher, i.e. 2% was undecided. There were 9 teachers, i.e. 18% who agreed tuition given by the teachers leads to different types of violence, 31, i.e. 62% disagreed and 10, i.e. 20% of the teachers were undecided. There are 35, i.e. 70% of the teachers who blamed partiality, prejudices and injustice done to the child by the parents, elders and teachers, 2, i.e. 4% of them disagreed with the statement and 13, i.e. 26% of the teachers were undecided. 27, i.e. 54% of the teachers agreed violence occurs more in uncongenial school environment, 8, i.e. 16% of the teachers disagreed and 15, i.e. 30% of them were undecided. 27, i.e. 54% of the teachers blamed lack of interest in school, 13, i.e. 26% disagreed and 10, i.e. 20% of the teachers were undecided.

In Champhai district, out of the 50 teachers, 20 teachers, i.e. 40% agreed that poor supervision of the school authorities has led to violence against girls in school and 29 teachers, i.e. 58% did not agree and 1 teacher, i.e. 2% is undecided. 35 teachers, i.e. 70% agreed that peer group influence acts as the common cause on violence amongst the students, 11 teachers, i.e. 22% disagreed with the statement and 4 teachers, i.e. 8% were undecided. There were 35 teachers, i.e. 70% who agreed that excessive use of mobile phones plays a role and 12 teachers, i.e. 24% disagreed with the statement and 3 teachers, i.e. 6% were undecided. 33 teachers, i.e. 66% agreed that the lack of discipline in the school is one of the reasons of violence against girls, and 17 teachers, i.e. 34% disagreed and 0 teacher, i.e. 0% was undecided. There were 40 teachers, i.e. 80% who blamed domestic conflict as one of the causes, 8 teachers, i.e. 16% disagreed and 2 teachers, i.e. 4% were undecided. 43 teachers, i.e. 86% agreed that violent behaviour exhibited by parents has a great influence in inducing violence, 5 teachers, i.e. 10% disagreed and 2 teachers, i.e. 4% were undecided. There were 30 teachers, i.e. 60% who blamed adolescence period, 14 teachers, i.e. 28% disagreed and 6, i.e. 12% of the teachers were undecided. 43 teachers, i.e. 86% agreed that imitation from mass media is one of the causing factors, 6, i.e. 12% of the teachers disagreed with the statement and one was undecided. There were 27, i.e. 54%

of teachers who agreed that the lack of recreational opportunities and facilities amounted to a moderately high degree of violence and 19, i.e. 38% of the teachers disagreed and 4, i.e. 8% of them were undecided. There were 31 teachers, i.e. 62% who agreed that absence of teachers causes violence, 18, i.e. 36% of the teachers disagreed with the statement and 1 was undecided. 40, i.e. 80% of the teachers agreed that lack of guidance and counselling leads to violence, 8, i.e. 16% of the teachers disagreed and 2 teachers, i.e. 4% were undecided. There were 21 teachers, i.e. 42% who agreed tuition given by the teachers leads to different types of violence, 25, i.e. 50% disagreed and 4, i.e. 8% of the teachers were undecided. There were 36, i.e. 72% of the teachers who blamed partiality, prejudices and injustice done to the child by the parents, elders and teachers, 10, i.e. 20% of them disagreed with the statement and 4, i.e. 8% of the teachers were undecided. 37, i.e. 74% of the teachers agreed violence occurs more in uncongenial school environment, 8,·i.e. 16% of the teachers disagreed and 5, i.e. 10% of them were undecided. 28, i.e. 56% of the teachers blamed lack of interest in school, 19, i.e. 38% disagreed and 3, i.e. 6% of the teachers were undecided.

In Kolasib District, out of the 50 teachers, 20 teachers i.e.40% agreed that poor supervision of the school authorities has led to violence against girls and 18 teachers, i.e. 36% did not agree and 12 teachers, i.e. 24% were undecided. 28 teachers i.e.56% agreed that peer group influence acts as the common cause on violence amongst the students, 16 teachers, i.e. 32% disagreed with the statement and 6 teachers, i.e. 12% were undecided. There were 34 teachers, i.e. 68% who agreed that excessive use of mobile phones as one of the causes of violence and 9 teachers, i.e. 18% disagreed with the statement and 7 teachers, i.e. 14% were undecided. 24 teachers, i.e. 48% agreed that the lack of discipline in the school is one of the reasons of violence against girls, and 19 teachers, i.e. 38% disagreed and 7 teachers, i.e. 14% were undecided. There were 30 teachers, i.e. 60% who blamed domestic conflict as one of the causes, 7 teachers, i.e. 14% disagreed and 13 teachers, i.e. 36% were undecided. Forty four teachers, i.e. 88% agreed that violent behaviour exhibited by parents has a great influence in inducing violence, two teachers, i.e. 4% disagreed and 4 teachers, i.e. 8% were undecided. There were 25 teachers, i.e. 50%

who blamed adolescence period, 15 teachers, i.e. 30% disagreed and 10, i.e. 20% of the teachers were undecided. 43 teachers, i.e. 86% agreed that imitation from mass media is one of the causing factor, 3, i.e. 6% of the teachers disagreed with the statement and 4, i.e. 8% of the teachers were undecided. There were 21, i.e. 42% of teachers who agreed the lack of recreational opportunities and facilities amounted to a moderately high degree of violence, 18, i.e. 36% of the teachers disagreed, and 11, i.e. 22% of them were undecided. There were 24 teachers, i.e. 48% who agreed that absence of teachers causes violence, 21, i.e. 42% of the teachers disagreed with the statement and 5, i.e. 10% of the teachers were undecided. 45, i.e. 90% of the teachers agreed that lack of guidance and counselling leads to violence, 4, i.e. 8% of the teachers disagreed and one teacher, i.e. 2% are undecided. There were 12 teachers, i.e. 24% who agreed tuition given by the teachers leads to different types of violence, 32, i.e. 64% disagreed and 6, i.e. 12% of the teachers were undecided. There were 31, i.e. 62% of the teachers who blamed partiality, prejudices and injustice done to the child by the parents, elders and teachers, 7, i.e. 14% of them disagreed with the statement and 12, i.e. 24% of the teachers were undecided. 28, i.e. 56% of the teachers agreed violence occurs more in uncongenial school environment, 13, i.e. 26% of the teachers disagreed and 9, i.e. 18% of them were undecided. 29, i.e. 58% of the teachers blamed lack of interest in school, 12, i.e. 24% disagreed and 9, i.e. 18% of the teachers were undecided.

Comparison Among the Four Districts

Regarding the study on whether the poor supervision of the school authorities has led to violence against girls in school or not, the perception of teachers on the two districts i.e., Aizawl and Mamit have higher positive responses whereas Champhai and Kolasib have slightly lower responses. The peer group influence as the common cause on violence amongst the students as perceived by the teachers in Champhai and Mamit districts were rather extremely high, the other district, i.e. Kolasib is slightly higher than Aizawl district and Aizawl district being quite low occupies the lowest position in this matter.

The teacher's perception of all the four districts on the question whether the excessive use of mobile phones as one of the causes of violence or not, the data is indicative that it is so. The districts of Champhai, Mamit and Kolasib have more or less high positive responses in this regard. Again Aizawl district is having the lowest but inference drawn from this too speaks of the positive nature i.e., the excessive use of mobile phones likely leads to violence.

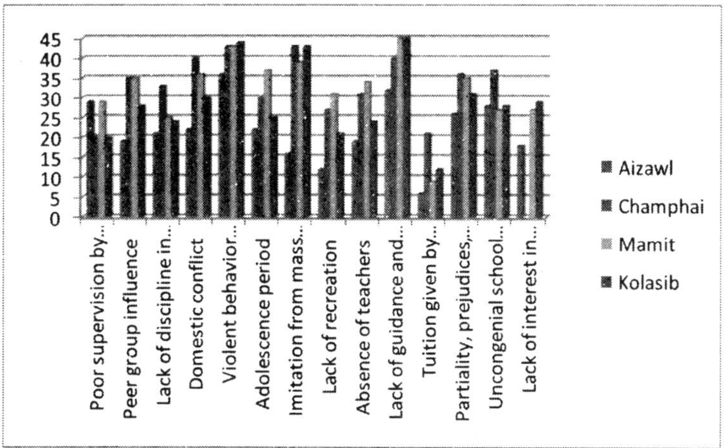

Fig. 4.6: Perceptions of Teachers on Violence against Girls

The respondent teachers from Champhai district think highly that the lack of discipline in the school is one of the reasons of violence against girls, the teachers of Mamit districts follow next, then Kolasib and then Aizawl district is having the lowest percentage.

The responses from the teachers of Champhai district scored highest when it comes to the perception that domestic conflict leads to violence among student. Next to Champhai district, the teachers from Mamit district score follows, then Kolasib district and Aizawl district teachers have the lowest score.

Respondent teachers from the entire four districts unequivocally perceived that violent behaviour exhibited by parents has a great influence in inducing violence. In this heading too, Aizawl district exhibits the lowest score amongst them.

In the three districts excepting low indication from Aizawl district, there is a unanimous response from the teachers that they believe that violence happened in secondary school because students are going through the adolescence period.

In the districts except for Aizawl, there is unanimously high score from the teacher respondents that violence against girls is enhanced by mass media and the imitation of improper and inappropriate behaviour from it.

In Mamit district, it is indicated that the teachers perceive the lack of recreational opportunities and facilities amounted to a moderately high degree of violence. In the same vein, Champhai district reveals a moderate percentage followed by Kolasib district with a little lower percentage. Even in this matter Aizawl district shows a very low percentage.

From the two districts of Champhai and Mamit, the data show that the teachers perceived that the absence of teachers from classroom makes students restless which in turn was a moderately contributing factor for violence. In Kolasib district slightly lower score than the previous two districts was revealed. In Aizawl district, the scenario inferred from the data indicates rather low percentage.

Lack of guidance and counselling is believed to be a major contributing factor for violence against girls in all the four districts under study—Mamit and Kolasib scoring extremely high followed by slightly lower Champhai. In this aspect, Aizawl district also has a moderately high percentage.

As regard to the question on violence among students as caused by partiality, prejudices and injustice done to the child by the parents, elders and teachers, the teachers from Champhai and Mamit perceived that this resulted in moderate degree of violence. Kolasib district data reveal that this aspect is also quite high and Aizawl district data too speak of a moderate state.

An inquiry into whether violence occurs more in uncongenial school environment, the respondent teachers of Champhai district viewed it as highly contributing factor. Even the other three districts exhibited moderate percentage in this aspect.

The three districts of Kolasib, Champhai and Mamit data show that the perception of teachers regarding the lack of interest in school is also a contributing factor for violence against girls. However, data from Aizawl district reveal a slightly lower percentage in this matter.

There were a few that were comparatively overt in contributing to violence against girls in secondary schools of Mizoram. The home which is the center of primary socialization has a proportionate effect on children in the manner they conduct themselves with regard to others in school. For obvious reasons, domestic conflicts and violent behaviour exhibited by parents at home reflect in school behaviour. On the next level, the influence of mass media, particularly the ones accessible through mobile phones, gets meshed in with peer pressure to steer students' behaviour in a certain way; and teachers feel that such inclinations are towards the negative. On the next level, teachers feel that all these factors do not get mitigated as there is a lack of guidance and counselling in the school environment.

On the whole teacher's perception of violence is none the less revealing. Teachers perceived that conflict at the domestic level, violent behaviour exhibited by parents and lack of proper guidance and counselling are the main causes of students turning violent, with girls becoming the natural victims. Thus, teachers attribute the negative effects of family socialization on the children which terminate in violent behaviour on the part of the teams and adolescents. All the districts under study are equivocal about the effect of negative socialization on the children. The teachers also continue to perceive that Peer Group influence, excessive use of mobile phones and imitable effect of mass media positively affect the violent behaviour of youth victimizing the girls in the secondary schools.

4.4 Perceptions of Parents on Violence against Girls

Family is the first school of citizenship. Parents are the most influential people in their children's lives. They absorb our words and actions. When they hear us say things that teach disrespect, they accept the ideas and values we often do not even realize we are transmitting. Now, if children see or hear us make excuses for disrespectful behaviours, does that mean that they will grow into disrespectful and violent people? Or that they will become victims of violence? Violence against girls is part of our world today, but there are many things parents can do to help prevent violence on girls. Homes and schools should be safe havens for children.

The Table 4.4 clearly indicates that, in Aizawl District out of the 50 parents, 29 parents, i.e. 58% agreed that poor supervision by the school authorities has led to violence against girls in school, and 17 parents, i.e. 34% did not agree and 4 parents, i.e. 8% were

Table 4.4: Parental Perception on Violence against Secondary School Girls

Sl. No.	Statement	Aizawl			Champhai			Mamit			Kolasib		
		Yes	No	UD	Yes	No	UD	Yes	No	UD	Yes	No	UD
1	Poor supervision by school authorities	18 — 36	19 — 38	13 — 26	18 — 36	13 — 26	19 — 38	30 — 60	10 — 20	10 — 20	27 — 54	16 — 32	7 — 14
2	Peer group influence	30 — 60	15 — 30	5 — 10	41 — 82	6 — 12	3 — 6	38 — 76	10 — 20	2 — 4	44 — 88	3 — 6	3 — 6
3	Excessive use of mobile phones	18 — 36	21 — 42	11 — 22	36 — 72	9 — 18	5 — 10	38 — 76	7 — 14	5 — 10	48 — 96	1 — 2	1 — 2
4	Lack of discipline in School	29 — 58	10 — 20	11 — 22	43 — 86	4 — 8	3 — 6	35 — 70	9 — 18	6 — 12	35 — 70	4 — 8	11 — 22
5	Domestic conflict	30 — 60	14 — 28	6 — 12	39 — 78	4 — 8	7 — 14	37 — 74	9 — 18	4 — 8	45 — 90	3 — 6	2 — 4
6	Violent behaviour exhibited by parents	41 — 82	8 — 16	1 — 2	41 — 82	7 — 14	2 — 4	37 — 74	11 — 22	2 — 4	44 — 88	5 — 10	1 — 2

(Contd.)

Sl. No.	Statement	Aizawl			Champhai			Mamit			Kolasib		
		Yes	No	UD	Yes	No	UD	Yes	No	UD	Yes	No	UD
7	Adolescence period	18 — 36	18 — 36	14 — 28	35 — 70	7 — 14	8 — 16	32 — 64	10 — 20	8 — 16	31 — 62	9 — 18	10 — 20
8	Imitation from mass media	33 — 66	12 — 24	5 — 10	47 — 94	2 — 4	1 — 2	45 — 90	3 — 6	2 — 4	41 — 82	3 — 6	6 — 12
9	Lack of recreation	17 — 34	24 — 48	9 — 18	30 — 60	14 — 28	6 — 12	29 — 58	12 — 24	9 — 18	22 — 44	18 — 36	10 — 20
10	Absence of teachers	23 — 46	18 — 36	9 — 18	31 — 62	7 — 14	12 — 24	37 — 74	8 — 16	5 — 10	42 — 84	5 — 10	3 — 6
11	Lack of guidance and counselling	40 — 80	5 — 10	5 — 10	35 — 70	3 — 6	12 — 24	40 — 80	7 — 14	3 — 6	42 — 84	7 — 14	1 — 2
12	Tuition given by teachers	12 — 24	31 — 62	7 — 14	14 — 28	12 — 24	24 — 48	17 — 34	24 — 68	9 — 18	38 — 76	5 — 10	7 — 14

(Contd.)

Sl. No.	Statement	Aizawl			Champhai			Mamit			Kolasib		
		Yes	No	UD	Yes	No	UD	Yes	No	UD	Yes	No	UD
13	Partiality, prejudices, injustice by elder people	$\frac{38}{76}$	$\frac{8}{16}$	$\frac{4}{8}$	$\frac{41}{82}$	$\frac{5}{10}$	$\frac{4}{8}$	$\frac{34}{68}$	$\frac{8}{16}$	$\frac{8}{16}$	$\frac{41}{82}$	$\frac{4}{8}$	$\frac{5}{10}$
14	Uncongenial school environment	$\frac{29}{58}$	$\frac{7}{14}$	$\frac{14}{28}$	$\frac{26}{52}$	$\frac{9}{18}$	$\frac{15}{30}$	$\frac{23}{46}$	$\frac{13}{26}$	$\frac{14}{28}$	$\frac{32}{64}$	$\frac{11}{22}$	$\frac{7}{14}$
15	Lack of interest in school	$\frac{19}{38}$	$\frac{19}{38}$	$\frac{12}{24}$	$\frac{29}{58}$	$\frac{14}{28}$	$\frac{7}{14}$	$\frac{35}{70}$	$\frac{8}{16}$	$\frac{7}{14}$	$\frac{37}{74}$	$\frac{10}{20}$	$\frac{3}{6}$

Note: The figure in the numerator indicate the percentage and that of the denominators indicate the corresponding number.

undecided. 19 parents i.e.38% agreed that peer group influence acts as the common cause on violence amongst the students, 24 parents, i.e. 48% disagreed with the statement and 7 parents, i.e. 14% were undecided. There were 20 parents, i.e. 40% who agreed that excessive use of mobile phones plays a role and 29 parents, i.e. 58% disagreed with the statement and 1 parent, i.e. 2% were undecided. 21 parents, i.e. 42% agreed that lack of discipline in the school is one of the reasons of violence against girls and 21 parents, i.e. 42% disagreed and 8 parents, i.e. 16% were undecided. There were 22 parents, i.e. 44% who blamed domestic conflict as one of the causes, 13 parents, i.e. 26% disagreed and 15 parents, i.e. 30% were undecided. 36 parents, i.e. 72% agreed that violent behaviour exhibited by parents has a great influence in inducing violence, 7 parents, i.e. 14% disagreed and 7 parents, i.e. 14% were undecided. There were 22 parents, i.e. 44% who blamed adolescence period, 10 parents, i.e. 20% disagreed and 18 parents, i.e. 36% of the parents were undecided. 16 parents, i.e. 32% agreed that imitation from mass media is one of the causing factor, 19, i.e. 38% of the parents disagreed with the statement and 15, i.e. 30% of the parents were undecided. There were 12, i.e. 24% of parents who agreed that the lack of recreational opportunities and facilities amounted to a moderately high degree of violence and 20, i.e. 40% of the parents disagreed and 18, i.e. 36% of them were undecided. There were 19 parents, i.e. 38% who agreed that absence of teachers causes violence, 23, i.e. 46% of the parents disagreed with the statement and 8, i.e. 16% of the parents were undecided. 32, i.e. 64% of the parents agreed that lack of guidance and counselling leads to violence, 12, i.e. 24% of the parents disagreed and 6 parents, i.e. 12% were undecided.

There were six parents, i.e. 12% who agreed that tuition given by the teachers leads to different types of violence, 29, i.e. 58% disagreed and 15, i.e. 30% of the parents were undecided. There were 26, i.e. 52% parents who blamed partiality, prejudices and injustice done to the child by the parents, elders and teachers, 12, i.e. 24% of them disagreed with the statement and 12, i.e. 24% of the parents were undecided. 28, i.e. 56% of the parents agreed that uncongenial school environment is one of the causes of violence, 10, i.e. 20% of the parents disagreed and 12, i.e. 24% of them were undecided. 18, i.e. 36% of the parents blamed lack of interest in school, 25, i.e. 50% disagreed and 7, i.e. 14% of the parents were undecided.

From Champhai district out of the 50 parents, 20 parents i.e. 40% agreed that poor supervision of the school authorities have led to violence against girls in school and 29 parents, i.e. 58% did not agree and one parent, i.e. 2% were undecided. 35 parents i.e.70% agreed that peer group pressure influences the act of violence against girls, 11 parents, i.e. 22% disagreed with the statement and 4 parents, i.e. 8% were undecided. There were 35 parents, i.e. 70% who agreed that excessive use of mobile phones plays a role and 12 parents, i.e. 24% disagreed with the statement and 3 parents, i.e. 6% were undecided. 33 parents, i.e. 66% agreed that lack of discipline in the school is one of the reasons of violence against girls and 17 parents, i.e. 34% disagreed. There were 40 parents, i.e. 80% who blamed domestic conflict as one of the causes, 8 parents, i.e. 16% disagreed and 2 parents, i.e. 4% were undecided.43 parents, i.e. 86% agreed that violent behaviour exhibited by parents has a great influence in inducing violence, 5 parents, i.e. 10% disagreed and 2 parents, i.e. 4% were undecided. There were 30 parents, i.e. 60% who blamed adolescence period, 14 parents, i.e. 28% disagreed and 6 parents, i.e. 12% of the parents were undecided. 43 parents, i.e. 86% agreed that imitation from mass media is one of the causing factor, 6, i.e. 12% of the parents disagreed with the statement and 1, i.e. 2% of the parents were undecided. There were 27, i.e. 54% of parents who agreed that the lack of recreational opportunities and facilities amounted to a moderately high degree of violence and 19, i.e. 38% of the parents disagreed and 4, i.e. 8% of them were undecided.

There were 31 parents, i.e. 62% who agreed that absence of teachers causes violence, 18, i.e. 36% of the parents disagreed with the statement and 1, i.e. 2% of the parents were undecided. 40, i.e. 80% of the parents agreed that lack of guidance and counselling leads to violence, 8, i.e. 16% of the parents disagreed and 2 parents, i.e. 4% were undecided. There were 21 parents, i.e. 42% who agreed that tuition given by the teachers leads to different types of violence, 25, i.e. 50% disagreed and 4, i.e. 8% of the parents were undecided. There were 36, i.e. 72% parents who blamed partiality, prejudices and injustice done to the child by the parents, elders and teachers, 10, i.e. 20% of them disagreed with the statement and 4, i.e. 8% of the parents were undecided. 37, i.e. 74% of the parents agreed that uncongenial school environment is one of the causes of violence, 8, i.e. 16% of the parents disagreed and 5, i.e. 10% of them were undecided. 28, i.e. 56% of the parents blamed lack of interest in school, 19, i.e. 38% disagreed and 3, i.e. 6% of the parents were undecided.

From Mamit district out of the 50 parents, 29 parents i.e. 58% agreed that poor supervision of the school authorities have led to violence against girls in school and 17 parents, i.e. 34% did not agree and 4 parents, i.e. 8% were undecided. 35 parents i.e.70% agreed that peer group pressure influences the act of violence against girls, 8 parents, i.e. 16% disagreed with the statement and 7 parents, i.e. 14% were undecided. There were 34 parents, i.e. 68% who agreed that excessive use of mobile phones plays a role and 5 parents, i.e. 10% disagreed with the statement and 11 parents, i.e. 22% were undecided. 25 parents, i.e. 50% agreed that lack of discipline in the school is one of the reasons of violence against girls and 15 parents, i.e. 30% disagreed and 10 parents, i.e. 20% were undecided. There were 36 parents, i.e. 72% who blamed domestic conflict as one of the causes, 6 parents, i.e. 12% disagreed and 8 parents, i.e. 16% were undecided. 43 parents, i.e. 86% agreed that violent behaviour exhibited by parents has a great influence in inducing violence, one parent, i.e. 2% disagreed and 6 parents, i.e. 12% were undecided. There were 37 parents, i.e. 74% who blamed adolescence period, 3 parents, i.e. 6% disagreed and 10 parents, i.e. 20% of the parents were undecided. 39 parents, i.e. 78% agreed that imitation from mass media is one of the causing factor, 7, i.e. 14% of the parents disagreed with the statement and 4, i.e. 8% of the parents were undecided.

There were 31, i.e. 62% of parents who agreed that the lack of recreational opportunities and facilities amounted to a moderately high degree of violence and 8, i.e. 16% of the parents disagreed and 11, i.e. 22% of them were undecided. There were 34 parents, i.e. 68% who agreed that absence of teachers causes violence, 12, i.e. 24% of the parents disagreed with the statement and 4, i.e. 8% of the parents were undecided. 45, i.e. 90% of the parents agreed that lack of guidance and counselling leads to violence, 4, i.e. 8% of the parents disagreed and 1 parent, i.e. 2% were undecided. There were 9 parents, i.e. 18% who agreed that tuition given by the teachers leads to different types of violence, 31, i.e. 62% disagreed and 10, i.e. 20% of the parents were undecided. There were 35, i.e. 70% parents who blamed partiality, prejudices and injustice done to the child by the parents, elders and teachers, 2, i.e. 4% of them disagreed with the statement and 13, i.e. 26% of the parents were undecided. 27, i.e. 54% of the parents agreed that uncongenial school environment is one of the causes of violence, 8, i.e. 16% of the parents disagreed and 15, i.e. 30% of them were undecided. 27, i.e. 54% of the parents blamed lack of interest in school, 13, i.e. 26% disagreed and 10, i.e. 20% of the parents were undecided.

From Kolasib district out of the 50 parents, 20 parents i.e. 40% agreed that poor supervision of the school authorities have led to violence against girls in school and 18 parents, i.e. 36% did not agree and 12 parents, i.e. 24% were undecided. 28 parents i.e. 56% agreed that peer group pressure influences the act of violence against girls, 16 parents, i.e. 32% disagreed with the statement and 6 parents, i.e. 12% were undecided. There were 34 parents, i.e. 68% who agreed that excessive use of mobile phones plays a role and 9 parents, i.e. 18% disagreed with the statement and 7 parents, i.e. 14% were undecided. 24 parents, i.e. 48% agreed that lack of discipline in the school is one of the reasons of violence against girls and 19 parents, i.e. 38% disagreed and 7 parents, i.e. 14% were undecided. There were 30 parents, i.e. 60% who blamed domestic conflict as one of the causes, 7 parents, i.e. 14% disagreed and 13 parents, i.e. 36% were undecided. 44 parents, i.e. 88% agreed that violent behaviour exhibited by parents has a great influence in inducing violence, 2 parents, i.e. 4% disagreed and 4 parents, i.e. 8% were undecided.

There were 25 parents, i.e. 50% who blamed adolescence period, 15 parents, i.e. 30% disagreed and 10 parents, i.e. 20% of the parents were undecided. 43 parents, i.e. 86% agreed that imitation from mass media is one of the causing factor, 3, i.e. 6% of the parents disagreed with the statement and 4, i.e. 8% of the parents were undecided. There were 21, i.e. 42% of parents who agreed that the lack of recreational opportunities and facilities amounted to a moderately high degree of violence and 18, i.e. 36% of the parents disagreed and 11, i.e. 22% of them were undecided.

There were 24 parents, i.e. 48% who agreed that absence of

teachers causes violence, 21, i.e. 42% of the parents disagreed with the statement and 5, i.e. 10% of the parents were undecided. 45, i.e. 90% of the parents agreed that lack of guidance and counselling leads to violence, 4, i.e. 8% of the parents disagreed and 1 parent, i.e. 2% were undecided. There were 12 parents, i.e. 24% who agreed that tuition given by the teachers leads to different types of violence, 32, i.e. 64% disagreed and 6, i.e. 12% of the parents were undecided. There were 31, i.e. 62% parents who blamed partiality, prejudices and injustice done to the child by the parents, elders and teachers, 7, i.e. 14% of them disagreed with the statement and 12, i.e. 24% of the parents were undecided. 28, i.e. 56% of the parents agreed that uncongenial school environment is one of the causes of violence, 13, i.e. 26% of the parents disagreed and 9, i.e. 18% of them were undecided. 29, i.e. 58% of the parents blamed lack of interest in school, 12, i.e. 24% disagreed and 9, i.e. 18% of the parents were undecided.

Comparison Among the Four Districts

Regarding the study on whether the poor supervision of the school authorities have led to violence against girls in school or not, the perception of parents on the two districts i.e. Aizawl and Mamit have higher positive response whereas Champhai and Kolasib have slightly lower responses. The parents of all the four districts perceive equivocally that peer group influence is the most dangerous common cause of violence amongst the students targeting girls in secondary schools of Mizoram.

The parents' perception in all the four districts on the question of the excessive use of mobile phones as one of the causes of violence, the data is indicative that it is so in all the districts except Aizawl. The districts of Champhai, Mamit and Kolasib have high positive responses indicating excessive use of smart phones as one of the causes of violence. Aizawl district has the lowest position as the parents tend to believe in positive influence of the excessive use of mobile phones as a functional necessity.

The respondent parents from Champhai district think highly that the lack of discipline in the school is one of the reasons of violence against girls, followed by teachers of Mamit, Kolasib and Aizawl districts respectively. Out of all the four districts, the responses from the parents of Champhai district scored highest when it comes to the perception that domestic conflict resulting in students being violence prone. Next to Kolasib district, the parents from Mamit district, Champhai district and Aizawl district have similar high score.

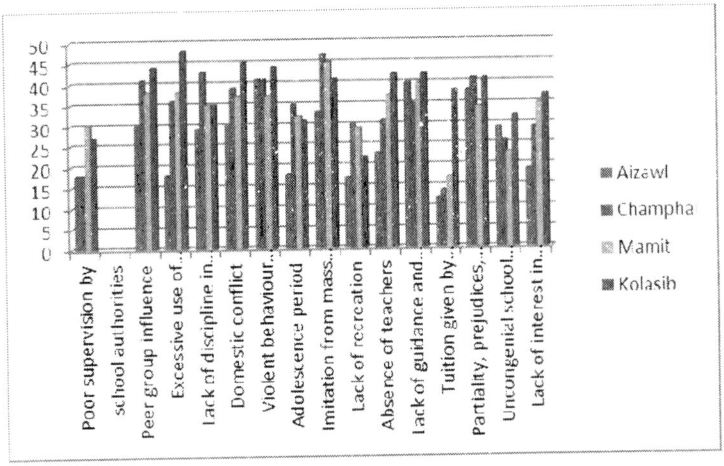

Fig. 4.7: Perceptions of Parents on Violence against Girls

Parents from the entire four districts unequivocally perceived that violent behaviour exhibited by parents has a great influence in inducing violence. In this regard, Mamit district scored the lowest, yet higher though all the other three districts exhibited the highest score.

In the districts except for Aizawl, there is unanimous response from the parents believing that violence happens in secondary school because of age-specific adolescence related personality disorder. The role of mass media in inducing violence can hardly be gainsaid. Out of the four districts, the parents tend to perceive that the violence against girls is enhanced by imitation of improper and inappropriate behaviour from mass media influence. Champhai and Kolasib scored the ever highest followed by Mamit and lowest yet higher by Aizawl district. In Mamit district, it is indicated that the parent's perception over the lack of recreational opportunities and facilities amounted to a moderately high degree of violence. In the same vein, Champhai district reveals moderate percentage followed by Kolasib district with a little lower percentage followed by Aizawl district.

From the two districts of Champhai and Mamit, the parents perceived that the absence of teachers from classroom makes students indisciplined which in turn moderately contributes to violence. In Kolasib district, responses were slightly lower than the said two districts, and in Aizawl, the scenario inferred from the data indicates rather low percentage. Lack of guidance and counselling is believed to be a major contributing factor for violence against girls in all the four districts under study. Mamit and Kolasib score extremely high followed by slightly lower score in Champhai. In this respect, Aizawl district also reveals a moderately high percentage.

In matters relating to tuition given by the teachers leading to different types of violence, the parents had low responses, of which Aizawl district was the lowest; the other two districts of Mamit and Kolasib had more or less the same low score. In Champhai district we have a slightly low or moderate scenario.

As regard to the question on violence among students as caused by partiality, prejudices and injustice done to the child by the parents, elders and teachers, the parents from Champhai and Mamit perceived that this resulted in highly moderate degree. Kolasib district data reveal that this aspect is also quite high and Aizawl district data too speak of a moderate response. An inquiry into whether violence occurs more in uncongenial school environment, the respondents of Champhai district viewed it as a high contributing factor. Even the other three districts exhibit moderate response in this respect.

The three districts of Kolasib, Champhai and Mamit data show that the perception of parents regarding the lack of interest in teacher-centred teaching learning is also a contributing factor for cross penetration of violence against girls. However, data from Aizawl district reveal a slightly lower percentage in this matter.

From the above analysis of the different perceptions of stake-holders, Teachers, parents and students—it is found that verbal assault is the most prevalent type of abuse against girls in the school. Parents and students perceive physical attack to be more common than name-calling and humiliation whereas teachers perceive physical attack to be much less common compared with students and the parents. All agree that abduction is the least experienced type of violence within the school. It should be noted that the percentages are generally above 30% and should also raise concerns. It also shows the level of perceived violence against girls on the way to and from school. The level of violence is perceived to be highest in Aizawl although generally, there are variations across regions in the perceptions of teachers, parents and students.

Teachers and students also agree that sexual harassment is frequent whereas parents believe humiliation and name-calling are more prevalent. Interview with the key informants and Focus Group Discussions (FGDs) with students, teachers and parents indicated that corporal punishment in the form of doing physically demanding jobs, forcing students to kneel down, twisting fingers/arms with pencils in between, pinching ears, flogging with rubber strings are common in schools. Such corporal punishment is perpetrated by teachers, school guards and principals when students (of both sexes) repeatedly engage in disruptive behaviour in the class, or fail to complete homework, or break rules and regulations or are late for school etc. During the field visits, the team observed the use of corporal punishments in almost every school visited. Paradoxically, the team came across several written statements written in bold face posted in school compounds, which talked about either the need to respect the rights of school children or about the need to eliminate corporal punishments. In one school, it read: "Corporal punishments in the schools should be abolished." Another board displayed: "We children need advice, not sticks." Another such slogan read: "Let's protect children from all forms of violence and exploitations." In practice, however, despite these impressive written slogans, the team witnessed girls facing corporal punishments. The team came across students who were forced to kneel down both inside and outside of classrooms. Seeing canes or small sticks in the hands of teachers, particularly of unit leaders and guards appeared to be the rule rather than exception. There was a tendency for principals and teachers to deny the existence of corporal punishment during the interviews and FGDs. Parents, particularly those who were members of Parent Teachers' Association also either denied or played down the existence of these forms of punishments in schools.

On the other hand, there were some reports of the trend of corporal punishment in schools declining. However, it was difficult to determine the truth of such claims as the issue fell outside the scope of the study. Parents and teachers also voiced their concern that, with no options for corporal punishment, teachers have become more passive and less able to maintain classroom discipline. This, parents and teachers reported, is not healthy for teacher student interaction which should be based on respect and mutual understanding.

4.5 Suggestions by Teachers

Teachers play a significant role in mitigating violence against girls in secondary schools. There are various ways of Suggested by teachers for the same. In Aizawl District, out of 50 teachers, 48 teachers, i.e. 96% agreed that schools should organize awareness programmes on non-violence and 2 teachers, i.e. 4% did not agree and 0 teachers, i.e. 0% was undecided. 48 teachers, i.e. 96% agreed that mobile phones should be restricted for students in school campus, 2 teachers, i.e. 4% disagreed with the statement and 0 teachers, i.e. 0% was undecided

There were 43 teachers, i.e. 86% who agreed that Peace education programme must be included in school curriculum and 3 teachers, i.e. 6% disagreed with the statement and 4 teachers, i.e. 8% were undecided. 35 teachers, i.e. 70% agreed that more time should be given to sports and other recreational activities on the curriculum and 7 teachers, i.e. 14% disagreed and 8 teachers, i.e. 16% were undecided. There were 40 teachers, i.e. 80% who agreed that girls at risk of being violent must be helped individually, 3 teachers, i.e. 6% disagreed and 7 teachers, i.e. 14% were undecided. 46 teachers, i.e. 92% agreed that guidance and counselling units should be established to help students with behavioural problems, 2 teachers, i.e. 4% disagreed and 2 teachers, i.e. 4% were undecided. There were 43 teachers, i.e. 86% who agreed that Parents should visit the school of their children from time to time to know their behaviour, 2 teachers, i.e. 4% disagreed and 5, i.e. 10% of the teachers were undecided. 45 teachers, i.e. 90% agreed that security arrangements should be made for school safety, 2, i.e. 4% of the teachers disagreed with the statement and 3, i.e. 6% of the teachers were undecided.

There were 37, i.e. 74% of teachers who agreed that girls should be taught self-defence through martial arts and 4, i.e. 8% of the teachers disagreed and 9, i.e. 18% of them were undecided. There were 44

Table 4.5: Suggestions of Teachers for Mitigating Violence against Girls in Secondary Schools

Sl. No.	Statement	Aizawl			Champhai			Mamit			Kolasib		
		Yes	No	UD	Yes	No	UD	Yes	No	UD	Yes	No	UD
1	Schools should organize awareness programmes on non-violence	49 — 98	1 — 2	0 — 0	49 — 98	1 — 2	0 — 0	50 — 100	0 — 0	0 — 0	50 — 100	0 — 0	0 — 0
2	Mobile phones should be restricted for students in school campus	50 — 100	0 — 0	0 — 0	49 — 98	0 — 0	1 — 2	49 — 98	1 — 2	0 — 0	49 — 98	0 — 0	1 — 2
3	Peace education programme must be included in school curriculum	46 — 92	3 — 6	1 — 2	41 — 82	2 — 4	5 — 10	42 — 84	1 — 2	7 — 14	43 — 86	3 — 6	4 — 8
4	More time should be given to sports and other recreational activities on the curriculum	38 — 76	5 — 10	7 — 14	42 — 84	4 — 8	4 — 8	35 — 70	5 — 10	10 — 20	36 — 72	6 — 12	8 — 16
5	Girls at risk of being violent must be helped individually	45 — 90	2 — 4	3 — 6	43 — 86	1 — 2	6 — 12	45 — 90	2 — 4	3 — 6	44 — 88	3 — 6	3 — 6

(Contd.)

Sl. No.	Statement	Aizawl			Champhai			Mamit			Kolasib		
		Yes	No	UD	Yes	No	UD	Yes	No	UD	Yes	No	UD
6	Guidance and counseling units should be established to help students with behavioural problems	47/94	2/4	1/2	48/96	1/2	1/2	50/100	0/0	0/0	48/96	0/0	2/4
7	Parents should visit the school of their children from time to time to know their behaviour	43/86	4/8	3/6	40/80	6/12	4/8	43/86	3/6	2/4	43/86	3/6	4/8
8	Security arrangements should be made for school safety	49/98	1/2	0/0	43/86	4/8	9/18	41/82	3/6	6/12	38/76	4/8	8/16
9	Girls should be taught self-defence through martial arts	36/72	3/6	11/22	37/74	4/8	9/18	40/80	2/4	8/16	38/76	4/8	8/16
10	Parent-teacher association should be established in every school	41/82	4/8	5/10	46/92	1/2	3/6	46/92	0/0	4/8	49/98	0/0	1/2

Note: The figures in the numerator indicate the percentage and that of the denominators indicate the corresponding number.

teachers, i.e. 88% who agreed that parent-teacher association should be established in every school, 3, i.e. 6% of the teachers disagreed with the statement and 3, i.e. 6% of the teachers were undecided.

In Champhai District, out of 50 teachers, 49 teachers, i.e. 98% agreed that schools should organize awareness programmes on non-violence and 0 teachers, i.e. 0% did not agree and 1 teacher, i.e. 2% were undecided. 48 teachers, i.e. 96% agreed that mobile phones should be restricted for students in school campus, 1 teacher, i.e. 2% disagreed with the statement and 1 teacher, i.e. 2% were undecided. There were 46 teachers, i.e. 92% who agreed that Peace education programme must be included in school curriculum and 0 teacher, i.e. 0% disagreed with the statement and 4 teachers, i.e. 8% were undecided. 42 teachers, i.e. 84% agreed that more time should be given to sports and other recreational activities on the curriculum and 4 teachers, i.e. 8% disagreed and 4 teachers, i.e. 8% were undecided.

There were 47 teachers, i.e. 94% who agreed that girls at risk of being violent must be helped individually, and 3 teachers, i.e. 6% were undecided. 46 teachers, i.e. 92% agreed that guidance and counselling units should be established to help students with behavioural problems, 1 teacher, i.e. 2% disagreed and 3 teachers, i.e. 6% were undecided. There were 44 teachers, i.e. 88% who agreed that Parents should visit the school of their children from time to time to know their behaviour, 0 teachers i.e.0% disagreed and 6, i.e. 12% of the teachers were undecided. 48 teachers, i.e. 96% agreed that security arrangements should be made for school safety, 0, i.e. 0% of the teachers disagreed with the statement and 2, i.e. 4% of the teachers were undecided. There were 37, i.e. 74% of teachers who agreed that girls should be taught self-defence through martial arts and 3, i.e. 6% of the teachers disagreed and 10, i.e. 20% of them were undecided. There were 46 teachers, i.e. 92% who agreed that parent-teacher association should be established in every school, 2, i.e. 4% of the teachers disagreed with the statement and 2, i.e. 4% of the teachers were undecided.

In Mamit District, out of the 50 teachers, 43 teachers, i.e. 86% agreed that schools should organize awareness programmes on non-violence and 1 teacher, i.e. 2% did not agree and 6 teachers, i.e. 12% were undecided. 47 teachers, i.e. 94% agreed that mobile phones should be restricted for students in school campus, 1 teacher, i.e. 2%

disagreed with the statement and 2 teachers, i.e. 4% were undecided. There were 48 teachers, i.e. 96% who agreed that Peace education programme must be included in school curriculum and 0 teachers, i.e. 0% disagreed with the statement and 2 teachers, i.e. 4% were undecided. 49 teachers, i.e. 98% agreed that more time should be given to sports and other recreational activities on the curriculum and 0 teacher, i.e. 0% disagreed and 1 teacher, i.e. 2% were undecided.

There were 46 teachers, i.e. 92% who agreed that girls at risk of being violent must be helped individually, 2 teachers, i.e. 4% disagreed and 2 teachers, i.e. 4% were undecided. 44 teachers, i.e. 88% agreed that guidance and counselling units should be established to help students with behavioural problems, 2 teachers, i.e. 4% disagreed and 4 teachers, i.e. 8% were undecided. There were 44 teachers, i.e. 88% who agreed that Parents should visit the school of their children from time to time to know their behaviour, 2 teachers, i.e. 4% disagreed and 4, i.e. 8% of the teachers were undecided. 46 teachers, i.e. 92% agreed that security arrangements should be made for school safety, 3, i.e. 6% of the teachers disagreed with the statement and 1, i.e. 2% of the teachers were undecided. There were 45, i.e. 90% of teachers who agreed that girls should be taught self-defence through martial arts and 2, i.e. 4% of the teachers disagreed and 3, i.e. 6% of them were undecided. There were 39 teachers, i.e. 78% who agreed that parent-teacher association should be established in every school, 2, i.e. 4% of the teachers disagreed with the statement and 9, i.e. 18% of the teachers were undecided.

In Kolasib District out of the 50 teachers, 38 teachers, i.e. 76% agreed that schools should organize awareness programmes on non-violence and 11 teachers, i.e. 22% did not agree and 1 teacher, i.e. 2% were undecided. 4 teachers, i.e. 86% agreed that mobile phones should be restricted for students in school campus, 2 teachers, i.e. 4% disagreed with the statement and 5 teachers, i.e. 10% were undecided. There were 48 teachers, i.e. 96% who agreed that peace education programme must be included in school curriculum and 2 teachers, i.e. 4% disagreed with the statement and 0 teachers, i.e. 0% was undecided. 46 teachers, i.e. 92% agreed that more time should be given to sports and other recreational activities on the curriculum and 2 teachers, i.e. 4% disagreed and 2 teachers, i.e. 4% were undecided.

There were 45 teachers, i.e. 90% who agreed that girls at risk of being violent must be helped individually, 3 teachers, i.e. 6% disagreed and 2 teachers, i.e. 4% were undecided. 49 teachers, i.e. 98% agreed that guidance and counselling units should be established to help students with behavioural problems, 1 teacher, i.e. 2% disagreed and 0 teacher, i.e. 0% was undecided. There were 48 teachers, i.e. 96% who agreed that Parents should visit the school of their children from time to time to know their behaviour, 1 teacher, i.e. 2% disagreed and 1, i.e. 2% of the teachers were undecided. 49 teachers, i.e. 98% agreed that security arrangements should be made for school safety, 1, i.e. 2% of the teachers disagreed with the statement and 0, i.e. 0% of the teachers were undecided. There were 46, i.e. 92% of teachers who agreed that girls should be taught self-defence through martial arts and 2, i.e. 4% of the teachers disagreed and 2, i.e. 4% of them were undecided. There were 43 teachers, i.e. 86% who agreed that parent-teacher association should be established in every school, 1, i.e. 2% of the teachers disagreed with the statement and 6, i.e. 12% of the teachers were undecided.

Comparison Among the Four Districts

Regarding the study on violence and the different suggestions made by the teachers, Aizawl and Champhai districts have higher positive response on whether schools should organize awareness programme on non-violence. Champhai and Kolasib have slightly lower responses. All four districts gave a very high response on the idea that suggested that mobile phones should be restricted for students in school campus.

The teachers' suggestion in all the four districts on whether peace education programme must be included in school curriculum or not, the data is indicative that it is necessary. The districts of Champhai, Mamit and Kolasib have more or less high positive responses in this regard. Aizawl district though positive has the lowest response. The respondent teachers from Mamit district suggest highly that more time should be given to sports and other recreational activities on the curriculum, the teachers of Kolasib districts follow next, then Champhai and Aizawl districts having the lowest percentage. Of all the four districts, the responses from the teachers of Champhai district scored highest when it came to the suggestion that girls at risk of being violent must be helped individually. Mamit district, Kolasib district and Aizawl district teachers have near similar opinion.

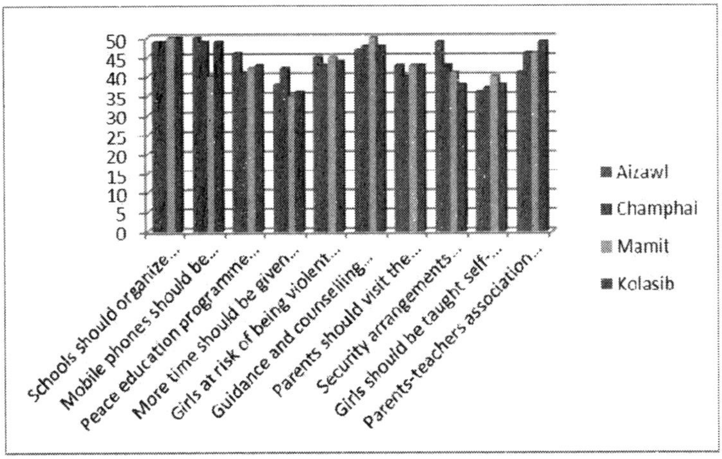

Fig. 4.8: Suggestions by teachers on Violence against Girls

Teachers from the four districts unequivocally perceived that guidance and counselling units should be established to help students with behavioural problems. In this heading, Champhai district exhibited the lowest score amongst them. In the four districts, there is a unanimous response from the teachers that they believe that parents should visit the school of their children from time to time to know their behaviour so as to decrease the chances of their kids being violent. Out of the four districts Kolasib scored the highest and Aizawl the lowest.

All the respondent teachers from the four districts strongly suggest that security arrangements should be made for school safety, with all four districts scoring above 90%. In regards with the topic of weather girls should be taught self-defence through martial arts or not, teachers from Kolasib scored the highest followed by Mamit, Champhai and Aizawl. Respondents from each of the four districts gave a more or less high score with regards to whether parent-teacher association should be more effective in every school.

4.6 Suggestions by Parents

From Table 4.6 it is found that, in Aizawl District, out of the 50 parents, 48 parents, i.e. 96% agreed that schools should organize

Table 4.6: Suggestions by Parents for Reducing Violence against Girls in Secondary Schools

Sl. No.	Statement	Aizawl			Champhai			Mamit			Kolasib		
		Yes	**No**	**UD**	**Yes**	**No**	**UD**	**Yes**	**No**	**UD**	**Yes**	**No**	**UD**
1	Schools should organize awareness programmes on non-violence	48 — 96	2 — 4	0 — 0	49 — 98	0 — 0	1 — 2	43 — 86	1 — 2	6 — 12	38 — 76	11 — 22	1 — 2
2	Mobile phones should be restricted for students in school campus	48 — 96	2 — 4	0 — 0	48 — 96	1 — 2	1 — 2	47 — 94	1 — 2	2 — 4	43 — 86	2 — 4	5 — 10
3	Peace education programme must be included in school curriculum	43 — 86	3 — 6	4 — 8	46 — 92	0 — 0	4 — 8	48 — 96	0 — 0	2 — 4	48 — 96	2 — 4	0 — 0
4	More time should be given to sports and other recreational activities on the curriculum	35 — 70	7 — 14	8 — 16	42 — 84	4 — 8	4 — 8	49 — 98	0 — 0	1 — 2	46 — 92	2 — 4	2 — 4
5	Girls at risk of being violent must be helped individually	40 — 80	3 — 6	7 — 14	47 — 94	0 — 0	3 — 6	46 — 92	2 — 4	2 — 4	45 — 90	3 — 6	2 — 4

(*Contd.*)

Sl. No.	Statement	Aizawl			Champhai			Mamit			Kolasib		
		Yes	**No**	**UD**	**Yes**	**No**	**UD**	**Yes**	**No**	**UD**	**Yes**	**No**	**UD**
6	Guidance and counseling units should be established to help students with behavioural problems	46/92	2/4	2/4	46/92	1/2	3/6	44/88	2/4	4/8	49/98	1/2	0/0
7	Parents should visit the school of their children from time to time to know their behaviour	43/86	2/4	5/10	44/88	0/0	6/12	44/88	2/4	4/8	48/96	1/2	1/2
8	Security arrangements should be made for school safety	45/90	2/4	3/6	48/96	0/0	2/4	46/92	3/6	1/2	49/98	1/2	0/0
9	Girls should be taught self-defence through martial arts	37/74	4/8	9/18	37/74	3/6	10/20	45/90	2/4	3/6	46/92	2/4	2/4
10	Parent-teacher association should be established in every school	44/88	3/6	3/6	46/92	2/4	2/4	39/78	2/4	9/18	43/86	1/2	6/12

Note: The figure in the numerator indicate the percentage and that of the denominators indicate the corresponding number.

awareness programmes on non-violence more often and 2 parents, i.e. 4% do not agree. 96% parents agreed that mobile phones should be restricted for students in school campus and 4% parents disagree with the statement.

It is seen from the above table that, there were 43 parents, i.e. 86% who agreed that Peace education programme must be included in school curriculum and 3 parents, i.e. 6% disagreed with the statement and 4 parents, i.e. 8% were undecided. 35 parents, i.e. 70% agreed that more time should be given to sports and other recreational activities on the curriculum and 7 parents, i.e. 14% disagreed and 8 parents, i.e. 16% were undecided. There were 40 parents, i.e. 80% who agreed that girls at risk of being violent must be helped individually, 3 parents, i.e. 6% disagreed and 7 parents, i.e. 14% were undecided. 46 parents, i.e. 92% agreed that guidance and counselling units should be established to help students with behavioural problems, 2 parents, i.e. 4% disagreed and again 2 parents, i.e. 4% were undecided.

There were 43 parents, i.e. 86% who agreed that Parents should visit the school of their children from time to time to know their behaviour, 2 parents, i.e. 4% disagreed and 5, i.e. 10% parents were undecided. 45 parents, i.e. 90% agreed that security arrangements should be made for school safety, 2, i.e. 4% of the parents disagreed with the statement and 3, i.e. 6% of the parents were undecided. There were 37, i.e. 74% of parents who agreed that girls should be taught self-defence through martial arts and 4, i.e. 8% of the parents disagreed and 9, i.e. 18% of them were undecided. There were 44 parents, i.e. 88% who agreed that parent-teacher association should be established in every school, 3, i.e. 6% of the parents disagreed with the statement and 3, i.e. 6% of the parents were undecided.

In Champhai district, out of the 50 parents, 49 parents, i.e. 98% agreed that schools should organize awareness programmes on non-violence and 0 parents, i.e. 0% does not agree and 1 parent, i.e. 2% were undecided. 48 parents, i.e. 96% agreed that mobile phones should be restricted for students in school campus, 1 parent, i.e. 2% disagree with the statement and 1 parent, i.e. 2% were undecided. There were 46 parents, i.e. 92% who agreed that Peace education programme must be included in school curriculum and 0 parents, i.e. 0% disagreed with the statement and 4 parents, i.e. 8% were undecided.

42 parents, i.e. 84% agreed that more time should be given to sports and other recreational activities on the curriculum and 4 parents, i.e. 8% disagreed and 4 parents, i.e. 8% were undecided.

There were 47 parents, i.e. 94% who agreed that girls at risk of being violent must be helped individually, and 3 parents, i.e. 6% were undecided. 46 parents, i.e. 92% agreed that guidance and counselling units should be established to help students with behavioural problems, 1 parent, i.e. 2% disagreed and again 3 parents, i.e. 6% were undecided. There were 44 parents, i.e. 88% who agreed that Parents should visit the school of their children from time to time to know their behaviour, and 6, i.e. 12% parents were undecided. 48 parents, i.e. 96% agreed that security arrangements should be made for school safety, 2, i.e. 4% of the parents were undecided. There were 37, i.e. 74% of parents who agreed that girls should be taught self-defence through martial arts and 3, i.e. 6% of the parents disagreed and 10, i.e. 20% of them were undecided. There were 46 parents, i.e. 92% who agreed that parent-teacher association should be established in every school, 2, i.e. 4% of the parents disagreed with the statement and 2, i.e. 4% of the parents were undecided.

In Mamit district, out of the 50 parents, 43 parents, i.e. 86% agreed that schools should organize awareness programmes on non-violence and 1 parent, i.e. 2% does not agree and 6 parents, i.e. 12% were undecided. 47 parents, i.e. 94% agreed that mobile phones should be restricted for students in school campus, 1 parent, i.e. 2% disagree with the statement and 2 parents, i.e. 4% were undecided. There were 48 parents, i.e. 96% who agreed that Peace education programme must be included in school curriculum and 0 parents, i.e. 0% disagreed with the statement and 2 parents, i.e. 4% were undecided. 49 parents, i.e. 98% agreed that more time should be given to sports and other recreational activities on the curriculum and 0 parents, i.e. 0% disagreed and 1 parent, i.e. 2% were undecided. There were 46 parents, i.e. 92% who agreed that girls at risk of being violent must be helped individually, 2 parents, i.e. 4% disagreed and 2 parents, i.e. 4% were undecided. 44 parents, i.e. 88% agreed that guidance and counselling units should be established to help students with behavioural problems, 2 parents, i.e. 4% disagreed and again 4 parents, i.e. 8% were undecided.

There were 44 parents, i.e. 88% who agreed that parents should visit the school of their children from time to time to know their behaviour, 2 parents, i.e. 4% disagreed and 4, i.e. 8% parents were undecided. 46 parents, i.e. 92% agreed that security arrangements should be made for school safety, 3, i.e. 6% of the parents disagreed with the statement and 1, i.e. 2% of the parents were undecided. There were 45, i.e. 90% of parents who agreed that girls should be taught self-defence through martial arts and 2, i.e. 4% of the parents disagreed and 3, i.e. 6% of them were undecided. There were 39 parents, i.e. 78% who agreed that parent-teacher association should be established in every school, 2, i.e. 4% of the parents disagreed with the statement and 9, i.e. 18% of the parents were undecided.

In Kolasib district, out of the 50 parents, 38 parents, i.e. 76% agreed that schools should organize awareness programmes on non-violence and 11 parents, i.e. 22% does not agree and 1 parent, i.e. 2% were undecided. 43 parents, i.e. 86% agreed that mobile phones should be restricted for students in school campus, 2 parents, i.e. 4% disagree with the statement and 5 parents, i.e. 10% were undecided. There were 48 parents, i.e. 96% who agreed that Peace education programme must be included in school curriculum and 2 parents, i.e. 4% disagreed with the statement and 0 parents, i.e. 0% was undecided. 46 parents, i.e. 92% agreed that more time should be given to sports and other recreational activities on the curriculum and 2 parents, i.e. 4% disagreed and 2 parents, i.e. 4% were undecided. There were 45 parents, i.e. 90% who agreed that girls at risk of being violent must be helped individually, 3 parents, i.e. 6% disagreed and 2 parents, i.e. 4% were undecided. 49 parents, i.e. 98% agreed that guidance and counselling units should be established to help students with behavioural problems, 1 parent, i.e. 2% disagreed and again 0 parent, i.e. 0% was undecided. There were 48 parents, i.e. 96% who agreed that Parents should visit the school of their children from time to time to know their behaviour, 1 parent, i.e. 2% disagreed and 1, i.e. 2% parents were undecided. 49 parents, i.e. 98% agreed that security arrangements should be made for school safety, 1, i.e. 2% of the parents disagreed with the statement and 0, i.e. 0% of the parents were undecided. There were 46, i.e. 92% of parents who agreed that girls should be taught self-defence through martial arts and 2, i.e. 4% of the parents disagreed and 2, i.e. 4% of them were undecided. There were 43 parents, i.e. 86% who agreed that parent-teacher association should be established in every school, 1, i.e. 2% of the parents disagreed with the statement and 6, i.e. 12% of the parents were undecided.

Comparison Among the Four Districts

Regarding the study on violence and the different suggestions made by the parents, Aizawl and Champhai district have higher positive response on whether schools should organize awareness programmes on non-violence; Mamit and Kolasib have slightly lower responses. All four districts gave high response on the idea that mobile phones should be restricted for students in school campus.

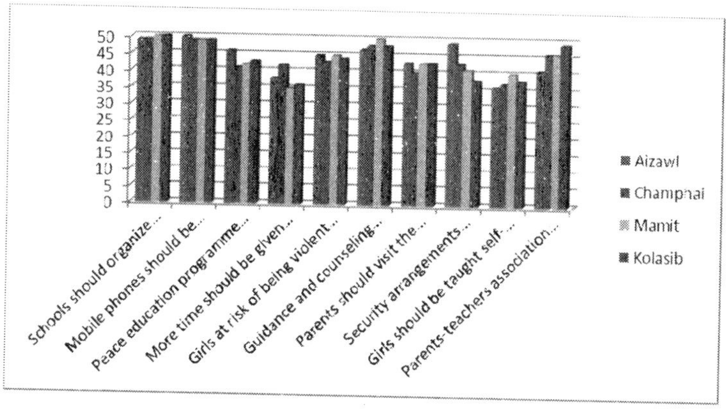

Fig. 4.9: Suggestions by Parents on Violence against Girls

The parents' suggestion of all the four districts on whether peace education programme must be included in school curriculum or not, the data is indicative that it should be included as evidenced from the responses of parents from Champhai, Mamit and Kolasib districts. The parents from Mamit district suggest highly that more time should be given to sports and other recreational activities on the curriculum, the teachers of Kolasib districts follow next. Of all the four districts, the responses from the parents of Champhai district scored highest when it came to the suggestion that girls at risk of being violent must be helped individually.

Parents from the entire four districts unequivocally perceived that guidance and counselling units should be established to help students with behavioural problems. In this heading, Champhai district exhibit the lowest score amongst them. In the four districts, there is a unanimous response from the parents that parents should visit the school of their children from time to time to know their behaviour so as to decrease the chances of their kids being violent. Out of the four districts Kolasib scored the highest and Aizawl the lowest. All the respondent parents from the four districts strongly suggest that security arrangements should be made for school safety, with all four districts scoring above 90%.

In regards with the topic of weather Girls should be taught self-defence through martial arts or not, parents from Kolasib scored the highest followed by Mamit, Champhai and Aizawl. Respondents from each of the four districts gave a more or less high score with regard to frequent parent-teacher association interaction in every school.

4.7 Effects of Violence and Abuse on Girls' Education

For this section, a qualitative based interview schedule was prepared with principals, headmasters and senior teachers in mind as respondents. We interviewed them on the topic of whether they had a 'no tolerance' to child abuse policy in their schools, and then asked them some follow up questions designed according to the possibilities of the answer being a high, low, moderate, and no effect.

It was found that none of the respondents had an official child abuse prevention policy in school. The reason for this was varied, and considered both the teacher and student as subjects. In the former case, it was felt that it is the responsibility of the teacher to understand the students' individual interests, habits, weakness etc. before giving any sort of punishment. The latter case was further varied and ranged from the thought that students can be disciplined without physical punishment and public humiliation in most cases; to the inverse effect of violence making them even more obstinate and hard-headed. Interestingly, none of the respondents felt that the no-tolerance policy was affected by the gender of the students.

We asked the respondents if the no-tolerance policy is in effect because the headmaster/principal says so, or because the teachers themselves are not willing. Most of the respondents felt that the no-tolerance policy is a result of both official and individual preferences. Not only are the teachers unwilling but they also agree that there are better and more humane forms of ensuring discipline, and that violence does not necessarily help in making better students as conformists. Only one respondent gave a subjective answer that violence on students depends upon the teacher and the teacher's point of view.

Interestingly, considering the unanimous take of the respondents on the negativity and ineffectiveness of violence, when we asked them if there were certain students who did deserve to receive a beating, only one respondent felt that no student ever deserved a beating since everyone must be treated with non-violent disciplinary action no matter howsoever is the deviant behavioural pattern. As against this, certain students went to contend that punishment in schools builds greater conformity and lesser deviance. However, they all did provide further explanation to this possible situation saying that unless otherwise very extremely necessary, violent methods be not resorted to either in school or in family.

We then asked their opinions on the general situation of violence against girls in secondary schools of Mizoram. We emphasised upon the possible positive and negative influences that physical punishment can have on girls and their education—keeping in mind their age requirements, social position, gender status and future prospects. One respondent made an observation regarding the nature of girls saying that since they get scared and frightened easily, a stern word is enough to discipline them and therefore violence in any form may have adverse effect on their psyche, motivation and academic achievement. One respondent felt that most of adolescent girls are generally better behaved by nature, and so enforcement of violence may bring shock and only ruin their future endeavour. Her opinion was furthered by the rest of the respondents who felt that negative influences can range from mental shock, decreased self-esteem and confidence, dropping out of schools and evoking even more unruly behaviour. One of the respondents presented an articulate observation that there are stray incidents of girls being beaten in other schools. It may be that the girl is exceedingly stubborn, or maybe the teacher is highly short tempered; but what is important here is that because of beating, the student may develop fear and not respect towards the teacher. One should know that being respected and being feared are two different factors which make a huge difference in the teaching profession. In general all respondents also made a case for gender equality, and that this kind of equality should be supplemented with treatment of love and care.

Box 6: Intimidation and Threat of Harm

A boy asked me to be his girlfriend. I refused the request. After few days, the same boy came running to me and showed me some pictures relating to sex. I paid a deaf ear. Asa result, the boy took a revenge on me repeatedly by stalking, insulting, threatening, and intimidating. Some of the words were very filthy and used with sexual intent: *Kamutpui duh che* (I want to sleep with you), *Tha ka ti lutuk che* (you are so beautiful), *min duhlo anih chuan tuman an neih bik lohna turin ka che ve ang* (I will block the way you go home. I was totally frightened and devastated. My worries and untold miseries continued long adversely affecting my education in general and my academic achievement in particular.

The qualitative data gathered through FGDs and key informant interviews indicate that violence and abuse against secondary school girls discourage parents from regularly sending their daughters to school because they are concerned about the safety of their adolescent daughters. This was mentioned by most of the parents who indicated that violence against school girls has a high discouraging effect on parents' motivation to send their daughters to school. Most parents of school girls whose daughters are threatened by boys do not allow their daughters to go to school because of fear of sexual abuse.

Any physical, sexual or psychological assault perpetrated against school girls is likely to exasperate their already low profile of educational participation thereby making them less and less visible in the school.

From Table 4.7, it is seen that most of the respondents are in favour of there is a direct impact of violence on girls' school absenteeism. Violence directly negatively affects girls' school attendance, their concentration, classroom activity and completion of homework, all of which are closely linked to their educational participation.

Table 4.7: Effects of Violence on Girls' School Absenteeism

Respondents	High (%)	Low (%)	Moderate (%)	No effect (%)
Students	64	21	12	3
Teachers	52	24	18	6
Parents	63	17	11	9

One of the immediate effects of violence on school girls is that it reduces their ability to attend classes. A girl who has been verbally abused or sexually harassed by her teacher is more likely to skip the teacher's class in order to avoid further abuse or harassment. Also a girl who has been sexually assaulted on the way to and from school is discouraged from going to school.

Box-7

A girl during the focus group discussions said that she is mostly preoccupied with fear of what would happen to her if she exposes her teacher's abusive behaviour. Having no hope she tolerates and pays attention to her studies.

Violence against secondary school girls reduces their ability to concentrate on their lessons. The presence of sexual or physical violence in the family or on the way to and from school has a destructive effect on school girls' concentration in the classroom. Female teachers who participated in focus group discussions noted that abused girls often become absent-minded in class and do not follow lessons attentively, most of the time draw blank when questions are asked or fumble—a sign of lack of concentration. Teachers further stated that some try to hide their heads (not to be identified) and become immersed in deep thoughts of what has happened at home or on the way to school. The presence of abusers (school boys or teachers) in the classroom creates a distressing experience on the part of school girls who watch their abusers living in freedom and peace, while the abused are suffering psychologically and emotionally.

In the FGD-1 teacher are commented that school girls are less likely to ask/answer questions in class compared to school boys who often are given priority in asking/answering questions. They often lag behind in completing class activities and having their work marked by teachers. The situation of school girls who have experienced sexual, physical or verbal violence and abuse is worse as such girls usually have limited or no motivation (lack of confidence, low moral, low self-esteem) to be involved in class activities.

Degrading comments and verbal insult by teachers and boys certainly do not encourage the participation of the girls. Also clever girls, who try to be active in the class, may face insults and harassment from their fellow male students. Active participation in class also requires regular class attendance and for the majority of abused school girls, it is very unlikely that they have been regularly attending class and hence they might miss some important lessons. This puts them in a disadvantaged position even when they try to do class activities.

The effects of certain types of violence on girls' class participation were assessed by cross tabulating the two and the results showed that school girls who experienced beating, excessive workload and rape more frequently assessed violence as highly contributing to girls' low-class participation.

4.7.1 *Being Unable to Complete Homework*

Any form of violence against school girls has a negative impact on their ability to complete school homework. This reduces their chances of getting good grades and lowers their educational participation. This is especially true of excessive workloads at home, which tends to consume their time and energy and hence little or no time for study and for doing assignments. Similarly, constant pestering of school girls has a destructive effect on girls' ability to complete homework. A girl who has been verbally abused or sexually harassed is not likely to be able to concentrate on her study and complete homework on time.

Table 4.8: Effects of Violence on Girls' Inability to Complete Homework

Respondents	High (%)	Low (%)	Moderate (%)	No effect (%)
Students	86	7	5	2
Teachers	79	8	11	2
Parents	42	27	12	19

Student respondents were asked about the impact of violence on their inability to complete homework and their educational participation. A good proportion of the respondents who attempted the question indicated that their inability to complete homework due to violence perpetrated against them or suffering of some form of abuse. Difference in the responses between teachers and students were observed, with a relatively high proportion of students showing their agreement of the strong link between violence perpetrated against them and their inability to complete homework which terminates in reduced educational participation of girls.

4.7.2 *Effects of Violence and Abuse on Girls' Academic Achievement*

Violence and abuse on school girls has a profoundly destabilizing effect on the education of girls. Girls who are victims of violence are more likely perform poorly in school, have problems of concentration on their academic work, and lose interest in school altogether, and dropout from school resulting in poorer academic achievement.

Table 4.9: Effect of Violence on Girls' Academic Achievement

Respondents	High (%)	Low (%)	Moderate (%)	No effect (%)
Students	72	23	5	–
Teachers	78	19	3	–
Parents	84	12	4	–

From the above table it is seen that different types of violence and abuse experienced by school girls highly affect their academic achievement. Girls who experienced violence and abuse tend to perform low in schools.

4.7.3 *Effects of Violence on Girls' Future Life*

Childhood represents a critical period in the history having its own implications for future. This is the period when a child is particularly sensitive to certain environmental experiences. Mental disturbance, low participation and academic achievement and drop-out from school may have a debilitating effect on future career prospects of a student and more so a girl child.

Table 4.10: Effects of Violence on School Girls' Future Life

Respondents	High (%)	Low (%)	Moderate (%)	No effect (%)
Parents	84	12	4	-
Students	71	22	7	-
Teachers	74	18	8	-

More than 80% parents and more than 70% teachers and students were of the opinion that violence highly affects girls' future life. In one of the FGD participants pointed out that, Teenage girls who are victimized tend to leave their area and migrate to nearby towns and some of them end up being commercial sex workers. Female teachers and key informants also thought that victim girls often face disapproval by family members, relatives and the community at large. They are considered misfits, incapable of managing their homes or properly performing household chores.They also noted that most rural school girls who are overburdened with excessive workload at home tend to run away from home to the nearby towns or urban centres. Most of those who run away end up being as therapist in SPAs or commercial sex workers. Sexual violence has damaging effects on the health of school girls. Especially it exposes girls to sexually transmitted diseases such as HIV/AIDS.

On the whole, it is found that the different types of violence and abuse against secondary school girls negatively affected their education in various interrelated aspects.The occurrence of violence and abuse in school, on the way to and from school and at home affect girls' access to education partly because of parents' fear and concern for the safety and security of girls.

4.8 Summary of the Interpretations

The review of literature revealed that in order to develop effective and comprehensive intervention programs, understanding the perceptions of violence held by members of relevant caregivers and vulnerable victims is essential. Thus, looking back to the objectives of the study, an attempt was made to look at (a) Students' Perceptions of Types of Violent Acts against Girls in Secondary Schools, (b) Perceptions of Teachers, (c) Perceptions of Parents, (d) Suggestions by Teachers,

(e) Suggestion by Parents, and (f) Effects of Violence and Abuse on Girls Education such as Completion of Homework, Academic Achievement and Effects on Future Life.

In general, the results of this study support the view that violent act against girls in secondary schools is of concern to students, teachers, and parents in the state of Mizoram. Moreover, participants mentioned several kinds of aggressive and violent behaviours that occur often in their schools including fighting, beating, bullying, verbally and physically threatening others, and vandalism. Gang involvement, poor parental supervision, school staff victimization of students, and enroot intimidation due to location of school were perceived as contributing factors to school violence.

Students, teachers, and parents revealed that violence had several directions in their school. Violence employed by school staff to girl students, boys to girls, teachers to girl students, and parents to school going children were frequently observed. All participants recognized violence in three forms as verbal, physical, and emotional in conformity with literature reviewed. There was no issue of religious violence as the stakeholders perceived that Mizo society is communitarian and there is religious discipline and tolerance. Verbal violence was viewed by the participants as cruel teasing, harsh language, and verbal intimidation. Fighting, beating, spanking, bullying, especially larger students pushing/hitting younger or weaker student, vandalism, and gang activity in school environment were emphasized as physical violence. The last one, emotional violence was defined by the participants as threatening students to motivate in school task, or comparing with other students and/or siblings, inviting girls by teachers to secluded environment for sexual abuse and unequal treatment of girls (gender discrimination) that were mostly employed by parents.

Gender differences were mentioned by all the participants in the sense that boys continue to employ more physical violence whereas girls employing more verbal retaliation. Besides, low self-esteem and lack of confidence, feeling worthless seemed to promote involving violent acts in schools. Moreover, participants indicated that introverted and silent girls who could not defend themselves became the victims of school violence. Participants reported that limited support and supervision along with lack of communication among family members seemed to be link to involving violent acts in school. Moreover, the results revealed that the contributing factors to school violence were interrelated. Some participants also discussed the role of domestic violence (parental verbal, emotional, and physical abuse), and alcohol or substance abuse among family members (especially fathers). Additionally, participants indicated that teachers also employed physical punishment such as, beating and insulting. In some cases, participants observed that school principals and colleagues tended to tolerate violence employed by teachers. It could be known that when victims and their parents could not cope with the situation they requested transfer to another school.

Numerous participants of this study voiced regarding the detrimental effects of violence against girls in schools and saw its role in denying girls their right to education. Any physical, sexual or psychological assault perpetrated against school girls is likely to exasperate their already low profile of educational participation thereby making them less and less visible in the school. The situation of school girls who have experienced sexual, physical or verbal violence and abuse is worse as such girls usually have limited or no motivation (lack of confidence, low morale, low self-esteem) to be involved in class activities. Degrading comments and verbal insult by teachers and boys certainly do not encourage the school participation of the girls. Also clever girls, who try to be active in the class, may face insults and harassment from their fellow male students.

Any form of violence against school girls has a negative impact on their ability to complete school homework. This reduces their chances of getting good grades and lowers their educational participation. A girl who has been verbally abused or sexually harassed is not likely to be able to concentrate on her study and complete homework on time. The students were showing their agreement of the strong link between violence perpetrated against them and their inability to complete homework which terminates in reduced educational participation of girls. Further, the study revealed that girls who are victims of violence are more likely perform poorly in school, have problems of concentration on their academic work, and lose interest in school altogether, and dropout from school resulting in poorer academic achievement. Accordingly, mental disturbance, low participation and academic achievement and dropout from school tend to have a debilitating effect on future career prospects of a student and more so a girl child. Teenage girls who are victimized tend to leave their area and migrate to nearby towns and some of them end up being commercial sex workers. Sexual violence has damaging effects on the health of school girls. Especially, it exposes girls to sexually transmitted diseases such as HIV/AIDS. Female teachers and key informants also thought that victim girls often face disapproval by family members, relatives and the community at large.

When participants were asked about the suggestions in order to prevent school violence on girls, almost all participants suggested that developing and implementing a school-based and culturally appropriate violence prevention programme by considering the needs and priorities of the school. They also added that school-parent collaboration should be enhanced in dealing with school violence by rejuvenating and Parent-Teacher Association. Most of the respondents felt that the no- tolerance policy is a result of both official and individual preferences. Not only the teachers unwilling but they also agree that there are better and more humane forms of ensuring discipline, and that violence does not necessarily help in making better students as conformists.

The suggestions given by the participants included several relevant points. Establishment of more welfare centres to correct violent behaviour, the provision of basic needs for children, opportunity for sports and other recreational activities, games, debate, excursions, club activities, visitation to schools by parents, establishment of Guidance and Counselling units, peace education programme included in school curriculum, training of teachers for peace education establishment of peace clubs and restriction of mobile phones are some of the strategies suggested for solving violence behaviour of children in schools.

A vital component of violence prevention efforts in schools is to conduct a needs assessment to obtain the perceptions about violence from students, parents, and teachers. Therefore, the purpose of this study was not only to investigate the students, teachers and parents perceptions about the school violence in Mizoram but also to identify the needs and concerns important to participants so that appropriate school-based violence prevention programme can be developed. In this context, there have been several international instruments, National and State specific laws and policies for the purpose of protection of girl child in particular. There is a need to take stock of and to evaluate the International, National and State specific policies, laws and instruments. Next chapter attempts such stock taking.

5
Evaluation of Policies and Strategies

Children constitute 44 per cent of India's population. Unfortunately, many of them survive in some of the most difficult circumstances, both while they live with their families and when they are out of a family setup living as orphans and destitute. Studies have shown how the difficult situations in which children find themselves put them to an even greater risk of getting exposed to anti-social influences.

The National Policy for Children, 1974, declared children to be a 'supreme national asset'. It pledged measures to secure and safeguard all their needs, declaring that this could be done by making wise use of available national resources. Unfortunately, ten successive Five-Year Plans have not allocated adequate resources to meet the needs of children. An exercise on child budgeting carried out by the Ministry of Women and Child Development revealed that total expenditure on children in 2005-06 in health, education, development and protection together amounted to a mere 3.86 per cent, rising to 4.91 per cent in 2006-07. However, the share of resources for child protection was abysmally low at 0.034 per cent in 2005-06 and remained the same in 2006-07. Available resources have also not been utilized effectively for achieving outcomes for children (GOI 2007:6). As a result, the status and condition of children have remained far from secure.

Harmful traditional practices like child marriage, caste system, and discrimination against the girl child, child labour and Devadasi tradition impact negatively on children and increase their vulnerability to abuse and neglect. Lack of adequate nutrition, poor access to medical and educational facilities, migration from rural to urban areas leading to rise in urban poverty, children on the streets and child beggars, all result in breakdown of families. Thus increase the vulnerabilities of children and exposes them to situations of abuse and exploitation. In order to provide an effective alternative system, Government has enacted the Juvenile Justice (Care and Protection of Children) Act 2000 and Amendment Act, 2006 and introduced schemes and programmes to take care of the needs of children deprived of care, protection, family support and basic services, as well as children who come in conflict with law.

Care and protection of children is recognized as basic to their survival and growth. For children found in the most vulnerable situations, a rights-based and professional approach to their protection, rehabilitation and restoration is mandatory. This expectation not only stems from India's international commitments by way of the UN Convention on the Rights of the Child and its Optional Protocols, but also as a Constitutional guarantee. It is the way forward for the Indian society, determined, as it is, to hand over the baton to children as they grow into adulthood.

Children constitute 17.34 per cent of Mizoram's total population. Mizoram may be a small state in terms of population and area, but the percentage of both child abuse and crimes committed by juveniles is quite high. The Ministry of Women and Child Development, Government of India in its "Study on Child Abuse: INDIA 2007" ranked Mizoram second in child abuse amongst the 13 states 2 of India covered under the study. The study found that "in four of these states, the percentage of physical abuse was alarmingly high, above 80 per cent. These states were Assam (84.65%), Mizoram (84.64%), Delhi (83.12%) and Uttar Pradesh (82.77%).

A "Study of Child Abuse in Mizoram" prepared by the Social Welfare Department and Aizawl-based NGO, Human Rights & Law Network (HLRN) on 27 October, 2012 revealed that children are not safe anywhere in the state as most cases of child sexual abuse were committed by relatives, friends and teachers of the victims (ACHR, 2013:1-2).

5.1 Plans and Policies by the Government

India is signatory to a number of international instruments and declarations pertaining to the rights of children to protection, security and dignity. It acceded to the United Nations Convention on the Rights of the Child (UN CRC) in 1992, reaffirming its earlier acceptance of the 1959 UN Declaration on the Rights of the Child, and is fully committed to implementation of all provisions of the UN CRC. In 2005, the Government of India accepted the two Optional Protocols to the UN CRC, addressing the involvement of children in armed conflict and the sale of children, child prostitution and child pornography. India is strengthening its national policy and measures to protect children from these dangerous forms of violence and exploitation.

India is also a signatory to the International Conventions on Civil and Political Rights, and on Economic, Social and Cultural Rights which apply to the human rights of children as much as adults. The Government of India is addressing the protection rights of children in India within the framework of the MDGs which India has committed to achieve by 2015. The Mid-Term appraisal report on the 10th Plan found that India is far from achieving the MDGs as the outcomes on most of the goals were off-track in 2005. Before going to National Laws and Policies, it is necessary to keep a record of International instruments on child protection. Three important International Instruments for the protection of Child Rights that India is signatory to, are:

(a) Convention on the Rights of the Child (CRC) adopted by the UN General Assembly in 1989, is the widely accepted UN instrument ratified by most of the developed as well as developing countries, including India. The Convention prescribes standards to be adhered to by all State parties in securing the best interest of the child and outlines the fundamental rights of children, including the right to be protected from economic exploitation and harmful work, from all forms of sexual exploitation and abuse and from physical or mental violence, as well as ensuring that children will not be separated from their families against their will.

(b) Convention on the Elimination of All Forms of Discrimination against Women (CEDAW) is also applicable to girls under 18 years of age. Article 16.2 of the Convention lays special emphasis on the prevention of child marriages and states that the betrothal and marriage of a child shall have no legal effect and that legislative action shall be taken by States to specify a minimum age for marriage.

(c) SAARC Convention on Prevention and Combating Trafficking in Women and Children for Prostitution emphasizes that the evil of trafficking in women and children for the purpose of prostitution is incompatible with the dignity and honour of human beings and is a violation of basic human rights of women and children.

5.2 National Policies and Legislations

The Fundamental Rights and Directive Principles of the Constitution of India provide the framework for child rights. Several laws and national policies have been framed to implement the commitment to child rights. The following plans and policies were found to be in effect in India in general and Mizoram in particular which are constitutional mandates or Central Government Acts and Policies and State specific Rules.

(a) *Constitution of India*

The Constitution of India recognizes the vulnerable position of children and their right to protection. Following the doctrine of protective discrimination, it guarantees in Article 15 special attention to children through necessary and special laws and policies that safeguard their rights. The right to equality, protection of life and personal liberty and the right against exploitation are enshrined in Articles 14, 15, 15(3), 19(1) (a), 21, 21(A), 23, 24, 39(e), 39(f) and reiterate India's commitment to the protection, safety, security and well-being of all it is people, including children.

Article 14: The State shall not deny to any person equality before the law or the equal protection of the laws within the territory of India;

Article 15: The State shall not discriminate against any citizen on grounds only of religion, race, caste, sex, place of birth or any of them;

Article 15(3): Nothing in this article shall prevent the State from making any special provision for women and children;

Article 19(1)(a): All citizens shall have the right (a) to freedom of speech and expression;

Article 21: Protection of life and personal liberty—No person shall be deprived of his life or personal liberty except according to procedure established by law;

Article 21A: Free and compulsory education for all children of the age of 6 to 14 years;

Article 23: Prohibition of traffic in human beings and forced labour—(1) Traffic in human beings and beggars and other similar forms of forced labour are prohibited and any contravention of this provision shall be an offence punishable in accordance with law;

Article 24: Prohibition of employment of children in factories etc. —No child below the age of fourteen years shall be employed to work in any factory or mine or engaged in any other hazardous employment;

Article 39: The state shall, in particular, direct its policy towards securing:

(e) that the health and strength of workers, men and women, and the tender age of children are not abused and that citizens are not forced by economic necessity to enter vocations unsuited to their age or strength; (f) that children are given opportunities and facilities to develop in a healthy manner and in conditions of freedom and dignity and that childhood and youth are protected against exploitation and against moral and material abandonment.

(b) *National Policies*

The major policies and legislations formulated in the country to ensure child rights and improvement in their status include:

- National Policy for Children, 1974
- National Policy on Education, 1986
- National Policy on Child Labour, 1987
- National Nutrition Policy, 1993

- Report of the Committee on Prostitution, Child Prostitutes and Children of Prostitutes and Plan of Action to Combat Trafficking and Commercial Sexual Exploitation of Women and Children, 1998
- National Health Policy, 2002
- National Charter for Children, 2004
- National Plan of Action for Children, 2005

(c) *National Legislations*

National legislations for protection of child rights in the country are:

- Guardian and Wards Act, 1890
- Factories Act, 1954
- Hindu Adoption and Maintenance Act, 1956
- Probation of Offenders Act, 1958
- Bombay Prevention of Begging Act, 1959
- Orphanages and Other Charitable Homes (Supervision and Control) Act, 1960
- Bonded Labour System (Abolition) Act, 1976
- Immoral Traffic Prevention Act, 1986
- Child Labour (Prohibition and Regulation) Act,1986
- Prevention of Illicit Traffic in Narcotic Drugs and Psychotropic Substances Act, 1987
- Pre-natal Diagnostic Techniques (Regulation and Prevention of Misuse) Act, 1994
- Persons with Disabilities (Equal Protection of Rights and Full Participation) Act, 2000
- Juvenile Justice (Care and Protection of Children) Act, 2000
- Commission for Protection of the Rights of the Child Act, 2005
- Prohibition of Child Marriage Act 2006

Some of the important legislations are discussed below (under each Act relevant sections have been enumerated):

(i) The Indian Penal Code

(a) Foeticide (Sections 315 and 316)
(b) Infanticide (Section 315)

(c) Abetment of Suicide: Abetment to commit suicide of minor (Section 305)

(d) Exposure and Abandonment: Crime against children by parents or others to expose or to leave them with the intention of abandonment (Section 317)

(e) Kidnapping and Abduction:
   - Kidnapping for extortion (Section 360)
   - Kidnapping from lawful guardianship (Section 361)
   - Kidnapping for ransom (Section 363 read with Section 384),
   - Kidnapping for camel racing etc. (Section 363)
   - Kidnapping for begging (Section 363-A)
   - Kidnapping to compel for marriage (Section 366)
   - Kidnapping for slavery etc. (Section 367)
   - Kidnapping for stealing from its person: under 10 years of age only (Section 369)

(f) Procurement of minor girls by inducement or by force to seduce or have illicit intercourse (Section 366-A)

(g) Selling of girls for prostitution (Section 372)

(h) Buying of girls for prostitution (Section 373)

(i) Rape (Section 376)

(j) Unnatural Sex (Section 377).

(ii) The Pre-natal Diagnostic Techniques (Regulation and Prevention of Misuse) Act, 1994

This is an Act for the regulation of the use of pre-natal diagnostic techniques for the purpose of detecting genetic or metabolic disorders, chromosomal abnormalities or certain congenital malformations or sex-linked disorders, and for the prevention of misuse of such techniques for the purpose of prenatal sex determination leading to female foeticide and for matters connected therewith or incidental thereto.

(iii) The Juvenile Justice (Care and Protection of Children) Act, 2000 as amended 2006, 2015 [Act 2 of 2016]

The Juvenile Justice (Care and Protection of Children) Act, 2000 is a comprehensive legislation that provides for proper care, protection and treatment of children in conflict with law and children in need of care and protection by catering to their development needs, and by adopting a child friendly approach in the adjudication and disposition of matters in the best interest of children and for their ultimate rehabilitation through various institutions established under the Act. It conforms to the UN Convention on the Rights of the Child, the UN Standard Minimum Rules for the Administration of Juvenile Justice (The Beijing Rules), 1985, the UN Rules for the Protection of Juveniles Deprived of their Liberty and all other relevant national and international instruments.

It prescribes a uniform age of 18 years, below which both boys and girls are to be treated as children. A clear distinction has been made in this Act between the juvenile offender and the neglected child. It also aims to offer a juvenile or a child increased access to justice by establishing Juvenile Justice Boards and Child Welfare Committees. The Act has laid special emphasis on rehabilitation and social integration of the children and has provided for institutional and non-institutional measures for care and protection of children. The non-institutional alternatives include adoption, foster care, sponsorship, and after care.

The following sections of the Act deal with child abuse:

Section 23: *Punishment for cruelty to juvenile or child*: The Act provides for punishment (imprisonment up to six months) if a person having the actual charge of, or control over, a juvenile or the child, assaults, abandons, exposes or willfully neglects him/her, causes or procures him/her to be assaulted, abandoned, exposed or neglected in any manner likely to cause such juvenile/child unnecessary mental or physical suffering.

Section 24: *Employment of Juvenile or Child for Begging*: The Act provides for punishment (imprisonment for a term which may extend to 3 years and fine) if a person employs or uses any juvenile/child for the purpose or causes any juvenile to beg.

Section 26: *Exploitation of Juvenile or Child Employee*: The Act provides for punishment (imprisonment for a term which may extend to 3 years and fine) if a person ostensibly procures a juvenile/child for the purpose of any hazardous employment, keeps him in bondage and withholds his earnings or uses such earning for his own purposes.

The Act also provides for rehabilitation programmes, foster care, open shelter, sponsorships, special homes and adoptions, and undertakes the registration and inspection of child care institutions. It also enacts penalties for intoxication and exploitation of the child, improper adoption procedures, human trafficking, use in militant groups, kidnapping and abduction; and also lays down strict rules for discouraging corporal punishments. The law has been more stringent after amendments in 2015.

(iv) The Protection of Children from Sexual Offences Act, 2012 (32 of 2012) with the Protection of Children from Sexual Offences Rules, 2012 by the Criminal Law (Amendment) Act, 2013 (13 of 2013)

Mizoram State Child Protection Society of the Social Welfare Department has issued booklets containing the details of the Act in both English and Mizo. The reason a Mizo version is available, is that not only it is more accessible for the local people, but also because it simplifies the legal jargon to everyday speech.

The booklet informs that sexual offences against minors can be categorized under "Penetrative Sexual Assault", "Aggravated Penetrative Sexual Assault", "Sexual Assault", "Aggravated Sexual Assault", and "Sexual Harassment"; with detailed explanation of what offenses imply. The punishments vary, depending upon the category, from 3 years to life imprisonment apart from fines levied.

The Act identifies usage of minors in pornography as a punishable crime with punishments which may extend up to 10 years apart from fines levied depending upon the level of participation of the perpetrator. These crimes and punishments are accorded to even those who participate at the level of abetment and, in much of the cases, the punishment of the abettor is similar to that of the actual perpetrator.

The Act lays down the various procedures for reporting of cases. Both the local police force and the Special Juvenile Police Unit are to take in any complaints and forward a report to the Child Welfare Committee within a period of 24 hours. Arrangements are also to be made in particular situations of providing a translator and also arrangements for care and protection during the investigation to the victim. Media, studios, and photographic facilities are obligated by law to aid in furnishing evidences for such investigations. Moreover, any person is also held accountable in cases where there has been a failure to report or failure to provide accurate information. Statements made by the minor victim have to be recorded by a magistrate, and arrangements are to be made for medical examinations. In order to a speedy trial, special courts are designated for the same.

(v) The Immoral Traffic (Prevention) Act, 1956

In 1986, the Government of India amended the erstwhile Suppression of Immoral Traffic in Women and Girls Act 1956 (SITA), and renamed it as the Immoral Traffic (Prevention) Act (ITPA) to widen the scope of the law to cover both the sexes exploited sexually for commercial purposes and to provide enhanced penalties for offences involving children and minors. "Child" under ITPA means a person who has not completed the age of sixteen years and "prostitution" means the sexual exploitation or abuse of persons for commercial purposes.

Section 3: Stringent action and punishment for keeping a brothel or allowing premises to be used as a brothel;

Section 4: Living on the earnings of prostitution;

Section 5: Procuring, inducing or taking a person for the sake of prostitution;

Section 6: If any person is found with a child in a brothel it shall be presumed, unless the contrary is proved, that he has committed an offence of detaining a person in premises where prostitution is carried on;

Section 6(1B): The punishment consists of imprisonment of either description for a term which shall not be less than 7 years, but which may be for life or for a term, which may extend to 10 years and shall also be liable to fine, with a provision for less than 7 years under special circumstances;

Section 6(2A): A child or minor found in a brothel, on medical examination, detected to have been sexually abused, it shall be presumed, unless the contrary is proved, that the child or minor has been detained for purposes of prostitution or, as the case may be, has been sexually exploited for commercial purposes;

Section 21: Establishment of Protective Homes by the State Government.

(vi) Child Labour (Prohibition and Regulation) Act, 1986

The Act was formulated to eliminate child labour and provides for punishments and penalties for employing children below the age of 14 years in from various hazardous occupations and processes. The Act provides power to State Governments to make Rules with reference to health and safety of children, wherever their employment is permitted. It provides for regulation of work conditions including fixing hours of work, weekly holidays, notice to inspectors, provision for resolving disputes as to age, maintenance of registers etc. Through a recent notification, child domestic workers up to 14 years of age working in hotels and *dhabas* have been brought within the purview of the Act. It is one step towards the total elimination of child labour.

(vii) The Prohibition of Child Marriage Act, 2006

The Child Marriage Restraint Act, 1929 has been repealed and the major provisions of the new Act include:

- Every child marriage shall be voidable at the option of the contracting party who was a child at the time of the marriage;
- The Court while granting a decree of nullity shall make an order directing the parties, parents and guardians to return the money, valuables, ornaments and other gifts received;
- The Court may also make an interim or final order directing the male contracting party to the child marriage or parents or guardian to pay maintenance to the female contracting party to the marriage and for her residence until her remarriage;
- The Court shall make an appropriate order for the custody and the maintenance of the children of child marriages;
- Notwithstanding that a child marriage has been annulled, every child of such marriage shall be deemed to be a legitimate child for all purposes;
- Child marriages to be void in certain circumstances like minor being sold for the purpose of marriage, minor after being married is sold or trafficked or used for immoral purposes etc.;

- Enhancement in punishments for male adults marrying a child and persons performing, abetting, promoting, attending etc. a child marriage with imprisonment up to two years and fine up to one lakh rupees; and
- States to appoint Child Marriage Prohibition Officers whose duties include prevention of solemnization of child marriages, collection of evidence for effective prosecution, creating awareness and sensitization of the community etc.

(viii) The Commissions for the Protection of Child Rights Act, 2005

The Act provides for the Constitution of a National and State Commissions for protection of Child Rights in every State and Union Territory. The functions and powers of the National and State Commissions will be to:

- Examine and review the legal safeguards provided by or under any law for the protection of child rights and recommend measures for their effective implementation;
- Prepare and present annual and periodic reports upon the working of these safeguards;
- Inquire into violations of child rights and recommend initiation of proceedings where necessary; Undertake periodic review of policies, programmes and other activities related to child rights in reference to the treaties and other international instruments;
- Spread awareness about child rights among various sections of society;
- Children's Courts for speedy trial of offences against children or of violation of Child Rights; State Governments and UT Administrations to appoint a Special Public Prosecutor for every Children's Court.

Apart from these laws mainly concerning children, there are a host of related social legislations and criminal laws which have some beneficial provisions for the care, protection and rehabilitation of children. The laws relating to commerce, industry and trade have some provisions for children, but they hardly provide any protection or cater to their developmental needs.

(d) *State Specific Rules and Policies: Mizoram*

ACHR (2013: 5) reported that there is an alarming increase in child abuse and crimes committed by the juveniles in Mizoram. According to official records, 89 cases of child abuse and 35 cases of children in conflict with law were registered in the state during January to March 2012. This included 76 cases of physical abuse and 13 cases of sexual abuse against minors registered by the Child Welfare Department, and 35 cases of children in conflict with law recorded by the Juvenile Justice Boards. Another shocking reality is the presence of a large number of children who are drug addicts. Human rights activists and officials agree that there could be around 10,000 to 30,000 child drug addicts in the state. According to Mizoram Social Defence & Rehabilitation Board Chief Executive Officer Lalparmawii, a survey had been conducted in 15 selected High Schools in Aizawl in which 470 students, including 227 girls, responded to the questionnaires and the survey found that drug abuse was rampant among the students (*Ibid*).

(i) *Self-Defence Centres*

Self-Défense Centre for Girl Child has been conducted in partnership with All Mizoram Karate Association (AMKA) and Mizoram Amateur Taekwondo Association (MATA). Experienced and qualified instructors were deployed by the Associations to each school, who cultivated sound cooperation with the schools. The students as well the teachers welcomed this programme. Positive feedback was received from all schools and the students.

(ii) *Kishori Shakti Yojana*

KSY aims at empowering adolescent girls so that they may become responsible citizens. It looks at all aspects of adolescent girl development. The large objective of the scheme is to advance the nutritional, health and development status of adolescent girls, support increasing knowledge of health, hygiene, nutrition and family care, and to integrate them with opportunities for learning life skills, going back to school, helping girls grow to understand their society and become prolific members of the society.

This scheme is a redesign of the already existing Adolescent Girls (AG) Scheme being implemented as a component under the centrally sponsored Integrated Child Development Services (ICDS) Scheme. The new scheme dramatically extends the coverage of the earlier scheme with significant content enrichment, strengthens the training component, particularly in skill development, aspects aimed at empowerment and enhanced self-perception. It also fosters convergence with other sectorial programmes, addressing the interrelated needs of adolescent girls and women. The scheme functions in the existing ICDS infrastructure. Under this scheme adolescent girls are offered non-formal education in life education aspects including physical, developmental and sex education. The girls are congregated at anganwadi centres. Girls can also be given basic health supplements such as IFA and de-worming tablets. Girls can also be given vocational training at the centres. The scheme now covers 5 districts—Lawngtlai, Champhai, Kolasib, Serchhip and Mamit Districts of Mizoram.

Objectives

(i) To provide the required literacy and numeric skills through the non-formal stream of education.
(ii) To stimulate a desire for more social exposure and knowledge and to help them improve their decision making capabilities.
(iii) To improve the nutritional, health and development status of adolescent girls, promote awareness on health, hygiene, nutrition and family care.
(iv) To link them to opportunities for learning life skills, to train and equip the adolescent girls to improve/upgrade home based and vocational skills.
(v) To help them gain a better understanding of their social environment and take initiatives to become productive members of the society.

Target Group: Adolescent Girls (11-18 yrs.)—both school going and out of school girls.

5.3 Activities of Integrated Child Protection Scheme in Mizoram

The Integrated Child Protection Scheme (ICPS) is a centrally Sponsored Scheme under the Ministry of Women and Child Development, with the primary aim of establishing a safety net of dedicated and quality personnel, structures and services for child protection across the country. In order to implement ICPS in Mizoram, MoU was signed between the Central and State Government on 30th April, 2010. The scheme aims to significantly contribute to the realization of Government/State responsibility for creating a system that will efficiently and effectively protect children by bringing several existing child protection programmes under one umbrella and integrates interventions for protecting children and preventing harm. It is based on cardinal principles of "protection of child rights" and "best interest of the child". The Scheme translates into programme, the vision of a secure environment for all children, as envisaged in the Juvenile Justice (Care and Protection of Children) Act, 2000, wherein their rights are ensured so that they can develop to their full potential.

The objective of the Scheme is "to provide a safe environment for the development and well being of children in difficult circumstances. It seeks to reduce vulnerabilities to situations and actions that lead to abuse, neglect, exploitation and separation of children from their families."

I. Setting Up of Mizoram State Child Protection Society

1. The Mizoram State Child Protection Society (MSCPS) has been set up *vide* Notification No. B. 12017/28/10-SWD dt. 26.8.2010 and registered under the Mizoram Societies Registration Act, 2005.
2. The State Project Support Unit has been set up *vide* Notification No. A. 11013/24/2010-SWD dt. 13.8.2010. Since the unit is to function at the initial phase of ICPS, the Unit has been phased out by the Ministry on 2015.
3. The Mizoram State Child Protection Society has State Child Protection Society and State Adoption Resource Agency at the state level and District Child Protection Unit at the district level.

II. Implementation Status of I.C.P.S.

The following table shows the status of various service delivery structures under Mizoram as per the Juvenile Justice (Care and Protection of Children) Act 2000, and ICPS Manual:

Table 5.1: Structure and Support Services in Mizoram as per Juvenile Justice (Care and Protection of Children), Act 2000

Sl. No.	Components	Present Status—Has the Structure been set up?
1	2	3
A. Service Delivery Structure		
(i)	State Child Protection Society (SCPS)	Yes
(ii)	State Adoption Resource Agency (SARA)	Yes
(iii)	District Child Protection Units (DCPU)	Yes (All 8 Districts)
(iv)	Child Guidance Centre	Yes (Aizawl District)
(v)	Childline	Yes (Aizawl & Mamit Districts)
B. Statutory Support Services		
(i)	Child Welfare Committees (CWCs)	Nos. set up—All 8 Districts
(ii)	Juvenile Justice Boards (JJBs)	Nos. set up—All 8 Districts
(iii)	Special Juvenile Police Units (SJPUs)	Nos. set up—All 8 Districts
C. Committees Formed		
1	State Advisory Board	Nos. set up—1
2	District Level Inspection Committee	Nos. set up—All 8 Districts
3	District Child Protection Committee	Nos. set up—All 8 Districts
4	Block Level Child Protection Committee	Nos. set up—26 RD Blocks
5	Village Level Child Protection Committee	Nos. set up—819 Villages
6	Sponsorship and Foster Care Approval Committee	Nos. set up—All 8 Districts
D. Existing Child Care Institutions		
1	Observation Home	Nos. set up—8 (Govt. Run)

(*Contd.*)

1	2	3
2	Special Home	Nos. set up—2 (Govt. Run)
3	Shelter Home	Nos. set up—5 (Govt. Run)
4	Children's Home	Nos. set up—29 (3 Govt. Run; 26 NGO Run)
5	Specialized Adoption Agency	Nos. set up—7 (1 Govt. Run; 6 NGO Run)

Source: Office Records of the Mizoram State Child Protection Society (MSCPS).

III. Statutory Support Services

1. Child Welfare Committee (CWC)

As the Juvenile Justice (Care and Protection of Children) Act, 2000 makes it mandatory to establish one *Child Welfare Committee* (*CWC*) in each district as the final authority to dispose of cases for the care, protection, treatment, development and rehabilitation of *Children in Need of Care and Protection* (*CNCP*) and to provide for their basic needs and protection of human rights, CWC has been established in all the eight districts of Mizoram. For effective functioning of CWCs, the scheme provides adequate infrastructure and financial support to the State Government.

Table 5.2: Cases Received by CWC of Mizoram

Sl. No.	**Status of CNCP produced before CWC**	**Jan. 2012 - March 2016**			**April 2016 - March 2017**		
		Boys	**Girls**	**Total**	**Boys**	**Girls**	**Total**
1	No. of cases on the first day	4	0	**4**	24	23	**47**
2	New CNCP cases presented	2515	2371	**4886**	510	554	**1064**

(*Contd.*)

Sl. No.	Status of CNCP produced before CWC	Jan. 2012 - March 2016			April 2016 - March 2017		
		Boys	Girls	Total	Boys	Girls	Total
3	No. of CNCP cases disposed	2495	2348	**4843**	507	536	**1043**
4	No. of CNCP pending cases	24	23	**47**	27	41	**68**

Source: Office Records of The Mizoram State Child Protection Society (MSCPS).

2. Juvenile Justice Board (JJB)

As the Juvenile Justice (Care and Protection of Children) Act, 2000 makes it mandatory to have one *Juvenile Justice Board (JJB)* in each district to deal with matters relating to *Children in Conflict with Law (CCL)*. JJB has been set up in all the eight districts of Mizoram. To facilitate setting up of JJB in each district and to ensure their effective functioning, the scheme provides adequate infrastructure and financial support to the State Government.

Table 5.3: Cases Received by JJB of Mizoram

Sl. No.	Status of CCL produced before JJB	Jan. 2012-March 2016			April 2016-March 2017		
		Boys	Girls	Total	Boys	Girls	Total
1	No. of cases on the first day	131	4	**135**	82	12	**94**
2	New CCL cases presented	1082	74	**1156**	331	16	**347**

(*Contd.*)

Sl. No.	Status of CCL produced before JJB	Jan. 2012-March 2016			April 2016-March 2017		
		Boys	Girls	Total	Boys	Girls	Total
3	No. of CCL cases disposed	1131	66	**1197**	326	23	**349**
4	No. of CCL pending cases	82	12	**94**	87	5	**92**

Source: Office Records of the Mizoram State Child Protection Society (MSCPS).

3. Special Juvenile Police Unit

As the Juvenile Justice (Care and Protection of Children) Act, 2000 provides for setting up Juvenile Police Units in every district to coordinate and upgrade the police interface with children, the Special Juvenile Police Units (SJPU) has been set up in all the eight Districts of Mizoram. All the police officers, designated as juvenile/child welfare officers in the district are members of the SJPU.

IV. Status of Children in Institutional Care in Mizoram

1. Observation Homes

Children in conflict with law who enter the juvenile justice system through the Juvenile Justice Board (JJB) are in need of adequate residential care and protection during the pendency of any inquiry regarding them under the Juvenile Justice (Care and Protection of Children) Act. The Act empowers the State Governments to establish and maintain either by itself or under an agreement with voluntary organizations, observation homes in every district or group of districts for their temporary reception [Sec. 8 (1) of the JJ Act, 2000]. In order to facilitate and expedite setting up of Observation Homes in every district or group of districts, the scheme provides financial support to the State Governments and Union Territory Administrations. There are 8 Government run Observation Homes in Mizoram.

Table 5.4: Details of Children in Observation Homes

Sl. No.	Details of Children	Jan. 2012 - March 2016			April 2016 - March 2017		
		Boys	Girls	Total	Boys	Girls	Total
1	No. of children on the first day	14	63	77	8	32	40
2	New children admitted	38	498	536	15	260	275
3	Children who have moved out	44	529	573	20	227	247
4	Number of children on the last day of the reported year/ month	8	32	40	3	65	68

Source: Office Records of the Mizoram State Child Protection Society (MSCPS)

2. Special Homes

Children in conflict with the law committed by the Juvenile Justice Board (JJB) for long term rehabilitation and protection require institutional services. The State Governments are empowered to establish

Table 5.5: Details of Children in Special Homes

Sl. No.	Details of Children	Jan. 2012 - March 2016			April 2016 - March 2017		
		Boys	Girls	Total	Boys	Girls	Total
1	No. of children on the first day	8	30	38	0	26	26
2	New children admitted	8	118	126	5	34	39
3	Children who have moved out	16	122	138	3	34	37
4	Number of children on the last day of the reported year/ month	0	26	26	2	24	26

Source: Office Records of The Mizoram State Child Protection Society (MSCPS).

and maintain either by itself or under an agreement with voluntary organizations, special homes in every district or group of districts for the reception and rehabilitation of juveniles in conflict with law. There are 2 Special Homes in Mizoram. One each in Aizawl and Lunglei and both Homes are Government run.

3. Shelter Homes

While a large number of urban marginalized children are in need of day care services, there are many others who require residential care for a temporary period for one or more reasons. These include children without parental care, run away children, migrant children etc. The State Government provides financial assistance to set up and administer Shelter Homes for such children. These Shelter Homes offer day and night shelter facilities to the children in need of support services for a temporary period, while efforts are made to rehabilitate them. In order to facilitate and expedite the setting up of Shelter Homes in every district or group of districts, the scheme provides financial support to the State Governments and Union Territories.

In Mizoram, there are 5 Government run Shelter Homes; one each in Aizawl, Mamit, Champhai, Lunglei and Saiha districts.

Table 5.6: Details of Children in Shelter Homes

Sl. No.	Details of Children	Jan. 2012 - March 2016			April 2016 - March 2017		
		Boys	Girls	Total	Boys	Girls	Total
1	No. of children on the first day	0	0	0	35	23	58
2	New children admitted	273	215	488	112	83	195
3	Children who have moved out	238	192	430	111	78	189
4	Number of children on the last day of the reported year/ month	35	23	58	36	28	64

Source: Office Records of The Mizoram State Child Protection Society (MSCPS).

4. Children's Homes

A large number of children in need of care and protection who enter the juvenile justice system through the Child Welfare Committee (CWC) are in need of residential care and protection during the pendency of any inquiry and subsequently for their long-term care, treatment, education, training, development and rehabilitation. The Juvenile Justice (Care and Protection of Children) Act, 2000 empowers the State Government either by itself or in collaboration with voluntary organizations to set up Children's Homes in every district or group of districts for the reception and residential care of such children. These homes served as a home away from home and provide comprehensive child care facilities to children for ensuring their all-round development. They work towards enhancing the capabilities and skills of children and work with their families with the view of facilitating their reintegration and rehabilitation into mainstream society.

There are 3 Government run Children's Homes (for Children with Special Needs) and 26 NGO run Children's Homes in Mizoram and all Homes received Grant-in-aid from Ministry of Women and Child Development through ICPS.

Table 5.7: Details of Children in Children's Homes

Sl. No.	Details of Children	Jan. 2012-March 2016			April 2016-March 2017		
		Boys	Girls	Total	Boys	Girls	Total
1	No. of children on the first day	520	696	1216	375	529	904
2	New children admitted	430	575	1005	108	158	266
3	Children who have moved out	575	742	1317	97	173	270
4	Number of children on the last day of the reported year/ month	375	529	904	386	514	900

Source: Office Records of the Mizoram State Child Protection Society (MSCPS).

5. Specialized Adoption Agencies (SAA)

In order to facilitate the placement of orphaned, abandoned and surrendered children for adoption, the Juvenile Justice (Care and Protection of Children) Act 2000 empowers the State Government to recognize one or more of its institutions or voluntary organizations in each district as SAA. Keeping in line with the provisions of the Act, the ICPS provides financial and other support to the setting up and functioning of SAAs in each district. The SAA provide quality childcare facilities to children including family based care during the pre-placement phase. SAA prepare individual care plan for each child following the principle of the best interest of the child.

The SAA works under the overall supervision of State Adoption Resource Agency and the District Child Protection Unit. There are 7 Specialized Adoption Agency (SAA); one is run by Government while the remaining three are run by NGO.

Table 5.8: Details of Children in Specialized Adoption Agencies

Sl. No.	Details of Children	April 2016 - March 2017		
		Boys	Girls	Total
1	No. of children on the first day	8	9	17
2	New children admitted	17	11	28
3	Children who have moved out	17	15	32
4	Number of children on the last day of the reported year/month	8	5	13

Source: Office Records of the Mizoram State Child Protection Society (MSCPS).

V. Status of Children in Non-Institutional Care in Mizoram

1. Adoption

In Mizoram, Adoption programme has been carried out with the establishment of Adoption Coordinating Agency (ACA). ACA was dissolved and converted into State Adoption Resource Agency in 2012. The following table shows the status of Adoption in Mizoram:

Table 5.9: Details of Children given for Adoption

Year	In-Country			Inter-Country		
	Girls	Boys	Total	Girls	Boys	Total
Before 2012	61	93	154	5	7	12
2012—2013	16	6	22	2	1	3
2013—2014	7	12	19	0	2	2
2014—2015	14	8	22	0	1	1
2015—2016	9	9	18	4	5	9
2016—2017	15	11	26	2	2	4
Grand Total	122	139	261	13	18	31

Source: Office Records of the Mizoram State Child Protection Society (MSCPS).

2. Foster Care

The scheme provides support for Foster Care through the Sponsorship and Foster Care Fund available with the District Child Protection Unit. The Child Welfare Committee either by itself or with the help of SAA, identifies suitable cases and order placement of the child in foster-care.

Table 5.10: Details of Children in Foster Care

Year	Total number of children on the last day of the year reported upon		
	Girls	Boys	Total
2012-2013	37	34	71
2013-2014	43	40	83
2014-2015	45	39	84
2015-2016	51	45	96
2016-2017	65	43	108

Source: Office Records of the Mizoram State Child Protection Society (MSCPS).

3. Sponsorship

ICPS creates a special Sponsorship and Foster Care Fund within the DCPU. Sponsorship offers supplementary financial support to families to meet the educational, medical, nutritional and other needs of children with a view to improving the quality of their lives.

Table 5.11: Details of Children in Sponsorship

Year	Total number of children on the last day of the year reported upon		
	Girls	Boys	Total
2012-2013	135	175	310
2013-2014	81	50	131
2014-2015	261	262	523
2015-2016	118	125	243
2016-2017	203	196	399

Source: Office Records of The Mizoram State Child Protection Society (MSCPS).

4. After Care

The Juvenile Justice (Care and Protection of Children) Act, 2000 provides for institutional care for juveniles in conflict with law and children in need of care and protection up to the age of 18 years. However, most of the children in care have nowhere to go once they reach the age of 18 and are discharged from their institutions. In addition, as empirically observed, institutional life does not prepare children well for life outside an institution. They are unable to sustain themselves and are easily affected by negative influences. There is a need to prepare these children to sustain themselves during the

Table 5.12: Details of Children in After Care

Year	Total number of children on the last day of the year reported upon		
	Girls	Boys	Total
2012-2013	10	10	20
2013-2014	10	10	20
2014-2015	16	13	29
2015-2016	17	28	45
2016-2017	3	6	9

Source: Office Records of the Mizoram State Child Protection Society (MSCPS).

transition from institutional to independent life. The District Child Protection Society is responsible to develop an After-care programme. Based on the case to case basis, the JJB/CWC passed placement order of a juvenile/child in the after-care programme.

5. Childline

It is the 24-hour toll-free emergency outreach service for children in need of care and protection. It provides emergency assistance to children and then links them to long term services for their care and rehabilitation. It works for the protection of the rights of all children between 0-18 years of age, but the special focus is on children in need of care and protection especially the more vulnerable sections. Any child/concerned adult on behalf of the child can dial 1098 and access the childline service any time of the day or night.

It was inaugurated in Aizawl through Centre for Peace and Development (CPD) in April 2011. CPD is the collaborative organization of CHILDLINE covering Aizawl and Mamit district. Besides responding to 1098 emergency calls, CHILDLINE Aizawl carries out advocacy, organizing workshops, outreach/awareness programmes and Open House for Children.

VI. Other Activities

1. Training/Awareness/Sensitization/Capacity Building etc. at State & District Level: State Child Protection Society, State Adoption Resource Agency and District Child Protection Units conducted training/awareness/capacity building programme etc. for various stakeholders including DCPU Staff, Child Welfare Committee, Juvenile Justice Board, Special Juvenile Police Unit, Medical personnel, staff of Child Care Institutions, Anganwadi Workers, College Lecturers, and NGOs etc. covering various topic related to child protection.

2. Track Child: Online data entry of all cases of children in Child Care Institutions, CWC, JJB & SJPU at Track Child Portal to trace missing and vulnerable children is an ongoing activity.

3. Operation Muskaan: A Campaign titled "Operation Muskaan" is conducted with the Police Department from 1st July, 2015 which will be a month long campaign. During this operation, all children residing in CCI, bus stand, road sides, markets, religious places, workshops, restaurants and tea stalls will be screened by the DCPU and Police Department. While screening cases of those children considered to be 'missing children' will be documented and necessary follow up action will be taken.

For the first part of the operation, Training was conducted on 29th June 2015 at Office of the Superintendent of Police, Aizawl District in which police personnel were given training on Laws and Acts related to Children.

4. Identification & Capacity Building of Nodal Teachers at Serchhip, Lawngtlai, Saiha, Champhai, Mamit and Lunglei to advocate child rights and all issues related to child protection.

5. Observation/Celebration of Child Related Days such as Children's Day (14th November), World Day for Prevention of Child Abuse (19th November), World Day against Child Labour (12th June) etc.

In observance of 'Child Abuse Prevention Month', the State Child Protection Society (SCPS) organized 'Child Abuse Prevention Awareness Exhibition' on 29th & 30th April, 2014 at Aizawl Club, Aizawl, and Mizoram. Using the theme *'Child Abuse Prevention'*, several competitions such as photography, poster, slogan, poetry and logo was conducted at the state level during March 2014.

6. Research and Documentation: The scheme facilitates carrying out comprehensive studies to assess the causes, nature and extent of specific child protection issues like trafficking and commercial sexual exploitation of children, violence against children etc. Following are the study conducted by SCPS:

(i) Baseline Survey and Need Assessment of Children in Mizoram—Collection of data, data entry finished. Write-up in progress.
(ii) Need Assessment of Child Care Institutions—Completed.
(iii) Profiling of Working Children in Mizoram- Completed.
(iv) Children Abusing Substance: A Situational Analysis—Completed.

7. IEC

(i) Hoardings: Displayed in every district.

(ii) Sponsoring of various Magazines and Local Events such as LPS Pro Fight 2014, LPS Health Tips, Mizoram Premier League, Mizoram Tennis Open, Inter-Veng Basketball Tournament, Cos Play etc.
(iii) Publication of Booklets: UNCRC, POCSO Act in Mizo language etc.
(iv) Publication of ICPS, JJB, CWC & Adoption leaflets and posters.
(v) Awareness/Advertisement by displaying ICPS video clips at Local channel.
(vi) Innovative Ads displayed at Millennium Centre and Local Channels.
(vii) ICPS and Child Protection Jingles at AIR, FM and local channels.

ICPS brings together multiple existing child protection schemes of the Ministry under one comprehensive umbrella, and integrates additional interventions for protecting children and preventing harm. ICPS, therefore, institutionalize essential services and strengthen structures, enhance capacities at all levels, create database and knowledge base for child protection services, strengthen child protection at family and community level, ensure appropriate inter-sectoral response at all levels.

The ICPS focus its activities on Children in Need of Care and Protection and Children in Conflict with Law as defined under the JJ Act and with children who come in contact with the law, either as victim or as a witness or due to any other circumstances. It also provides preventive, statutory and care and rehabilitation services to any other vulnerable child. Beyond this, ICPS also outlines the need for human resource development for strengthening counselling services, training and capacity building, strengthening the knowledge-base, conduct research studies, create and manage a child tracking system, carry out advocacy and public education programmes, and monitoring and evaluation of the scheme.

Child Protection has been an emerging issue in India including the state of Mizoram. Even though the existence of the Mizoram State Child Protection Society (MSCPS) is very new among the Mizo society, it achieved a great milestone in creating awareness on

Child Rights and other issues related to child protection. Before the setting up of MSCPS, many cases remain unreported and proper precautions were not taken to ensure the rights of children. With the implementation of ICPS in the State, there is an increased access to a wider range and better quality of protection services; increased investment in child protection and is continuously drawing focus on the right of all children to be safe.

(iv) Juvenile Justice in Mizoram

The functioning of the Child Welfare institutions in Mizoram providing access to juvenile justice requires substantive improvement (ACHR, 2013: 14-15).

(a) Status of the Juvenile Justice Boards Section 4, sub-section (1) of the JJ (C&PC) Act (as amended in 2006) provides that Juvenile Justice Boards (JJBs) should be constituted in every district within a period of one year from the date of commencement of the JJ (C&PC) Amendment Act, 2006, by notification in the Official Gazette. But Mizoram government was able to establish JJBs in all the eight districts only in 2010-11, with the inception of ICPS in Mizoram. Before 2010, the JJB at Lunglei used to cover three districts namely Lunglei, Saiha and Lawngtlai district.

The JJBs sit regularly once every week and also sit according to the number of case availability. At the 39th PAB meeting held on 15 March 2012 to discuss the financial proposal for release of grants for 2011-12 under ICPS for Mizoram, the PAB noted that only 79 cases have been taken up by JJBs during 2011 and two sittings per week of JJBs may not be required. The State Government reported that it reviewed the functioning of JJBs itself.

At the 43rd PAB Meeting under ICPS held on 6th July, 2012, the state government of Mizoram informed that pendency at the JJBs was high and number of sittings needed to be increased.

(b) Status of the Child Welfare Committees with the inception of ICPS in Mizoram, the Child Welfare Committees (CWCs) were established in all the eight districts of the State since 2010-11. However, before 2010, the CWC at Aizawl used to cover five districts including Aizawl, Champhai, Kolasib, Serchhip, and Mamit while the CWC at Lunglei used to cover three districts including Lunglei, Saiha and Lawngtlai.

At the 43rd PAB Meeting under ICPS held on 6th July 2012 to discuss the financial proposal for release of grants for 2012-13 under ICPS for Mizoram, the state government of Mizoram informed that CWCs and JJBs have been constituted and trained in all the 8 districts. The data entry operators have been appointed in all CWCs and JJBs from January this year. All the CWCs and JJBs have been provided with necessary furniture and equipment.

The State government reported that the CWCs sit for two days a week. There were 19 cases pending at the last day of the quarter in 2011-12.

It is alleged that although the CWCs have been established in all districts of the State, it is found that the CWC members hardly attend training programmes organized by the government. Moreover, they are busy workers and do not have time for the CWCs.

(c) *Inspection Committees*: At the 43rd PAB Meeting under ICPS held on 6th July 2012 to discuss the financial proposal for release of grants for 2012-13 under ICPS for Mizoram, the state government of Mizoram informed that only 31 inspections have been undertaken since 2007 when seven out of the eight inspection committees were formed. The State government informed that CWCs were carrying out frequent inspections of the Homes. The PAB advised Mizoram to activate the inspection committees as per the JJ(C&PC) Act and State JJ Rules and regular inspections, including surprise visits, should be undertaken. The State was also advised to form Management Committees for each Child Care Institution to oversee the day-to-day management of the Homes.

But ACHR (2013) has found that in a number of juvenile justice homes, there is hardly any inspection. The State Inspection Team has conducted only one inspection at Government Observation Home-cum-Special Home at Aizawl since its establishment in 1986 and no inspection has been done by the State Inspection Team at Government Observation Home-cum-Special Home at Lunglei since its inception in 2008. There has not been any inspection from the State Inspection Team or Mizoram State Child Protection Society (MSCPS)/ District

Child Protection Society (DCPS) officials at the three new established government-funded Shelter Homes at Aizawl, Mamit and Champhai.

(d) *Special Juvenile Police Units*: Section 75 of the Mizoram JJ Rules 2010 stipulates that while dealing with a juvenile or a child under the provisions of the Act and the rules made thereunder, except at the time of arrest, the police officials shall wear plain clothes and not the police uniform. But this is rarely followed in Mizoram.

Moreover, the Juvenile/Child Welfare Officers are hardly given training on child rights and JJ (C&PC) Act. All the designated Juvenile/Child Welfare Officers are police officers who receive training from the District Child Protection Society. However, in reality the police personnel who handled the juveniles are non-officers who did not receive training. Moreover, the designated Juvenile/Child Welfare Officers are often transferred to different posts, and a fresh training has to be given to the newly appointed Juvenile/Child Welfare Officers.

5.4. Framework for Reducing Violence against Girls in Secondary School

With this a list of international instruments, National and State specific laws and policies is brought in order. A vital component of violence prevention efforts in schools is to conduct a needs assessment to obtain the perceptions about violence from students, parents, and teachers. Therefore, the purpose of this study was not only to investigate the students, teachers and parents perceptions about the school violence in Mizoram but also to identify the needs and concerns important to participants so that appropriate school-based violence prevention programme can be developed.

In the context of Mizoram, it appears that there are glaring gaps in the infrastructure, set up and outreach services for children, as they exist now. Mechanism of protection of violence against girl students studying in secondary schools are not in order and do require to be streamlined. Thus, a framework of policy for protection of crime against girl students studying in secondary schools is given below so as to be able to tackle the problem effectively.

The framework of the project is structured around the adolescent girl whose age group falls under the senior secondary school category. Here we see four major structures surrounding her.

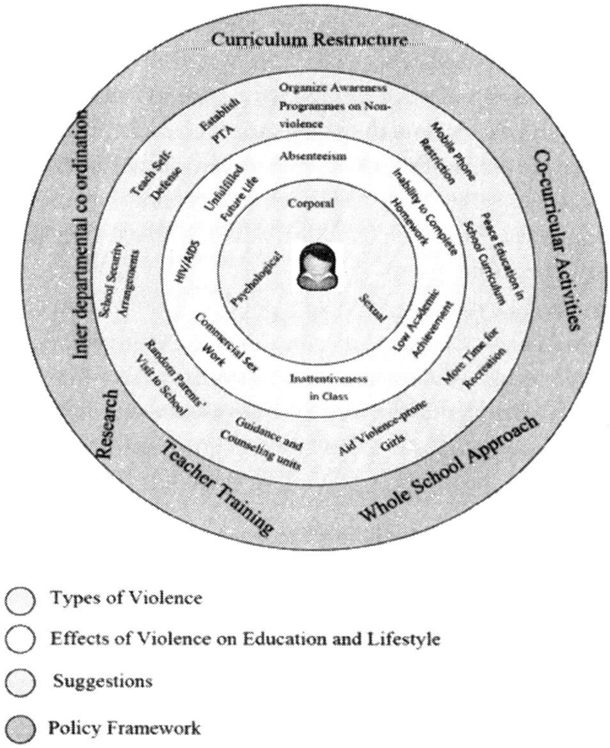

Fig. 5.1: Framework of violence against girls in secondary schools

1. The inner most circle represents the types of violence. Gender-based violence is a major problem where girls are sexually harassed or abused by their classmates or teachers. Tolerance of gender-based violence in schools is a serious form of discriminatory treatment that compromises the learning environment and educational opportunities for girls. Different types of violence like, Corporal, Sexual, and Psychological violence are seen in secondary schools.
   (a) *Corporal Violence*: This violence can be best defined as when a person uses force/violence with the intention of causing physical pain on the punished. Students are exposed to corporal punishment as a form of discipline. Being spanked, slapped, hit, shaken, pushed, kicked,

beaten or belted—these are all forms of violence teachers or school administrators inflict on their students. The high incidence of corporal punishment in schools is a clear indicator of the absence of use of positive disciplining techniques by teachers. The state government in Mizoram and other states in the country have banned corporal punishment in schools. However, corporal punishment continues unchecked. There is a need for formulating an implementable legislation banning corporal punishment and creating a system where in such cases are not only reported but strict action taken against abusive teachers and principals.

(b) *Sexual Violence*: Sexual violence is a sexual act committed against the person without their consent or by using force to fulfil their sexual desires and fantasies. There can be different types of sexual violence like completed force penetration, attempted force penetration, touching of their private areas. Psychological violence is also present in schools, where children may fear being belittled, humiliated, threatened or ridiculed by staff and peers. When coerciveness is used at home or at school sometimes it often leads to negative impact as the teachers often used threats or force their students. Many a time's children often feel unsafe in their schools or on their way to and fro. Many such students are victims of, or witnesses to, interpersonal violence, bullying and aggressive behaviour. Bullying is one of the most common type of violence which can be found at school, it is carried out through verbal or physical act that can inflict harm and suffering. With the advancement in technology Cyber-bullying has often become the source of violence through Text messages, email and social media. Though digital channels can provide a positive space for girls, they also present dangers and new avenues for violence to take place.

(c) *Psychological Violence*: Psychological violence was found in the form of verbal abuse, mental abuse, and emotional maltreatment. It includes acts or the failures to act by parents or caregivers that caused or could cause, serious behavioural, cognitive, emotional, or mental trauma. This can include parents, teachers and caregivers using extreme and/or bizarre forms of punishment, such as confinement for long periods of time or threatening or terrorizing a girl child. Less severe acts, but no less damaging, are belittling or rejecting treatment, using derogatory terms to describe the child, habitual tendency to blame the child or make her a scapegoat.

2. The second inner circle relates to effects of violence on education and lifestyle. Although all girls dream of going to schools without fear of being abused sadly this is not the reality for millions of students especially for girls. School violence is sadly a growing global phenomenon. Any physical, sexual or psychological assault perpetrated against school girls is likely to exasperate their already low profile of educational participation thereby making them less and less visible in the school. The situation such as degrading comments and verbal insult by teachers and boys, terminates in limited or no motivation (lack of confidence, low moral, low self-esteem) to be involved in class activities. The intelligent girls, who are active in the class face insults and harassment from their fellow male students. Students who are bullied are more likely than their peers to be depressed, lonely, or anxious and have low self-esteem. Bullies often act aggressively out of frustration, humiliation, anger and in response to social ridicule.

   Gender-based violence not only acts to discourage girls from going to school but may also cause parents to prohibit their daughters from attending school for fear that they too will be victimized.

   Accordingly, mental disturbance, low participation and academic achievement and drop out from school tend to have a debilitating effect on future career prospects of a student and more so a girl child. Teenage girls who are victimized tend to leave their area and migrate to nearby towns and some of them end up being commercial sex workers. Sexual violence has damaging effects on the health of school girls. Especially, it exposes girls to sexually transmitted diseases such as HIV/AIDS. Female teachers and key informants also thought that victim girls often face disapproval by family members, relatives and the community at large.

Thus, when a girl experience different kinds of violence, it affects her with Absenteeism, Inability to Complete Homework, Inattentiveness in Class, and Low Academic Achievement which results in Unfulfilled Future Life involving Commercial Sex Work and HIV/AIDS. They are abused by their families or peers and even their teachers at school which create long term effect on their physical and mental health.

3. The suggestions from the participants have been consolidated at the third inner circle. While major challenges are inevitable whenever an education system is expanded rapidly, one can still ask the question: are the strategic policy and political objectives focused on the right things? At present, in Mizoram and elsewhere in the country, much of the focus is on the provision of educational inputs, such as classrooms, laboratories, books and teachers, rather than violence free school and learning outcomes. Since the evidence shows that the inputs are not being translated into action, there is a need to realign focus system-wide on achieving violence free school and learning outcomes with due political commitments thereto. Establishment of more welfare centres to correct violent behaviour, the provision of basic needs for children, opportunity for sports and other recreational activities, games, debate, excursions, club activities, visitation to schools by parents, establishment of Guidance and Counselling units peace education programme included in school curriculum, training of teachers for peace education establishment of peace clubs and restriction of mobile phones are some of the strategies suggested for solving violence behaviour of children in schools. In order curb the violence against girls and to improve the situation for girls in secondary schools, Schools should organize awareness programmes on non-violence, Mobile phones should

be restricted for students in school campus, Peace education programme must bc included in school curriculum, More time should be given to sports and other recreational activities on the curriculum, Girls at risk of being violent must be helped individually, Guidance and Counselling units should be established to help students with behavioural problems, Parents should visit the school of their children from time to time to know their behaviour, Security arrangements should be made for school safety, Girls should be taught self-defence through martial arts, and Parent-teacher association should be established in every school.

4. Policy Framework structure is given at the extreme outer circle. The government's contribution is needed in the form of policies which may help prevention of violence on girls through Curriculum Restructuring, Co-curricular Activities, Whole School Approach, Teacher Training, Interdepartmental Coordination, Capacity building of Parents and Research.
   (a) *Curriculum Restructuring and Co-curricular Activities:* The framework requires non-formal education curriculum to engage young people in efforts to prevent and end violence against girls. It may provide young people with tools and expertise to understand the root causes of violence in their communities, to educate and involve their peers and communities to prevent such violence, and to learn about where to access support if violence is experienced. The peer educators may help deliver age-appropriate sessions. One group may start out with storytelling and games that may prompt them to think about gender bias and stereotypes, while others can organize poster competitions or develop local community-based campaigns and projects to address specific forms of violence against girls. The same can be adapted to national context, translated into local languages, and rolled out in schools and communities in partnership with child sensitive organizations. Curricula for both school students and teacher training institutes need to be revised to include specific transformative content to enable

recognition of the 'everyday acts' of gender stereotyping, and building capacity to challenge them. This may help addressing curricular outcomes for developing interpersonal skills, with emphasis on empathy, self-esteem, assertiveness, safety, and problem solving.

(b) *Whole School Approach*: The entire school community must come together to agree on a strong and clear message that violence, sexual harassment, bullying and intolerance are unacceptable in the school environment. A school-wide approach to safety and belonging sends a strong message to all individuals in the school community. A continued collaborative process that encourages a safe and caring climate addresses concerns related to harmful behaviours, including bullying, violence, threat, intimidation, and harassment. The process involves planning for and monitoring of change. When everyone is aware of the different ways that violence occurs, the people it affects and its impact, finding solutions will be much easier. The whole school approach model identifies the different activities that need to be delivered in an education setting to develop a whole school approach to preventing gender-based violence. It also considers the key players who need to be engaged—children and young people, teachers and staff, parents and community members. The model is made up of six key areas.

- Learning to understand Violence against Girls, challenge gender inequality and build respectful relationships and prevent future violence;
- Safeguarding to support people that experience forms of Violence against Girls;
- Participating to actively prevent Violence against Girls;
- Campaigning to take action to stop Violence against Girls which involves raising awareness across the organisation and joining local campaigns;
- Localising to work in relevant expert partnerships which involves Working with external experts and Building partnerships; and

- Institutionalising to embed a comprehensive prevention programme which involves changing the culture of the organisation and developing policies to stop Violence against Girls.

Teacher Training

It is essential to ensure high quality teacher training (both scientific and pedagogical) in the implementation of the restructured curriculum. teachers' training colleges should:

(a) Increase instruction of future teachers on gender equity, including lessons on the harms of sexual violence and harassment in the school environment as a discriminatory impediment to education, and develop ways to intervene to stop sexual harassment before it escalates to violence;
(b) Develop in-service training programmes for experienced teachers on the prevention of, and response to, sexual violence and harassment in their schools. Offer these workshops throughout the country. Appoint a faculty member within each teacher training college to coordinate training and research efforts on gender based violence; and
(c) Educate teachers on their responsibilities under any code of conduct that is developed.

Copies of the POCSO and Juvenile Justice Act and Rules printed in local language need to be circulated among all concerned and further to ensure that copies are kept in School libraries and community centres. Teachers trained can be trainers elsewhere.

Interdepartmental Coordination

Neither the national nor the state departments of education systematically monitor incidents of violence in schools. Elimination of violence against girls in schools requires interdepartmental coordination among all line departments, service providers and duty bearers. Such interdepartmental coordination has a lot of positive functions. It reduces or eliminates duplication of or gaps in services: Coordination builds trust and decreases competition and conflict. It shares information and the lessons learned from the experiences of others. Thus, coordination enlarges the scope of activities Violence prevention plans need to be developed in broad consultation and cooperation which are more likely to succeed than those prepared by a single group of professionals acting alone. There is a need to identify roles and responsibilities of each line department and to inform them such as Police, Health, Education, W and CD Department of concerned state as the nodal department, District Administration, Law and Civil Society through policy notification. This can be accomplished by arranging training and Sensitization programmes for all functionaries in coordination.

Capacity building of Parents

Including parents in the whole-school approach to safety of their girl children has an enormous impact on the school climate and on students' relationships with each other. The relationship between positive school climate and family involvement is reciprocal: each builds on the other. Strengthening the involvement of parents in school leads to overlapping spheres of influence between home, school, and the community. Importance of Parent -Teacher Association's (PTA'S) is recognized everywhere.Parent-teacher partnerships are developmental in nature, promoting cooperation between home and school and having a positive impact on the attitudes of students, teachers, and the parents themselves. Parental involvement in planning promotes cooperation between home and school, which in turn fosters improved student academic achievement, behaviour, and self-concept. Parents and teachers collaborating on the school-wide plan for violence free school share a common basis for action. Sustained effort and commitment will secure the partnership's success. Specifically, assisting parents in the development of parenting skills that support constructive relationships with their children can be beneficial in ensuring attachment security and healthy development. Securely attached children experience their parents as being available and responsive to their needs. This security fosters adaptive exploration and buffers children from stress.

Preparing families to share the problem and to work collaboratively with the school to solve it is an important first step for practitioners. Active listening will help to foster a trusting relationship and help the family to feel accepted and understood. It can contribute to establishing a helping relationship and is a useful way to gain information and understand what the family and young person are experiencing. Parents can also be encouraged to use active listening skills as a way to support young people and parents to talk or continue talking. Conversations will validate whether there is a bullying problem that needs to be addressed, and will help identify options and determine an appropriate course of action. While young people are often reluctant to talk about bullying, taking an interest in the young person's school and friends is one way of facilitating the conversation.

The school must encourage faculty to solicit as much parental involvement as possible. Among the ways this can be achieved are school/class newsletters, classroom activities, web sites, personalized phone calls, local newspapers, voice mail direct to teachers, and opportunities for participation in school clubs, organizations, and other extracurricular activities. There are some innovative ways to increase the extent to which students and parents/guardians connect with their school, faculty, and staff. Examples include having parent advisory meetings, using parents/guardians as mentors and/or guest speakers, providing parents/guardians attending school functions with childcare for their children, establishing a parent lounge, and offering parenting classes.

Capacity building of Parents thus may include: (i) letting parents know about the education programme, when it is happening and what will be talked about, this could be through sending home leaflets and support details, (ii) sending home discussion notes for parents to talk about with their children, (iii) inviting parents to participate in family workshops that develop relationships and encourage good communication between parents and children, (iv) deliver workshops and courses for parents, see the section on parents learning, and (v) listening to parents' views through surveys and research.

Research

The problem of school violence is multi-faceted and can be understood to include violence perpetrators, victims of violence, feelings of fear and insecurity, criminal and antisocial behaviour, and the disciplinary system established by the school. Various prevention and intervention programmes and ideas regarding violence against girl child in schools in particular and society in general are changing over time. Research is needed to examine the effectiveness of these programmes over time and across cultural, gender, and geographic lines so as to make proper assessment of vulnerabilities towards devising actionable strategies. Further work should also focus on threat assessment, the potential for an offener to commit a violent act targeting a girl child. It is then critical that this research becomes readily available for policy-makers, treatment providers, individuals associated with juvenile justice systems, and the general public. Once preventative programmes are in place, and more research has been conducted concerning their effectiveness, a better understanding of school violence and ways in which to lessen its impact can be determined. The Government may support research to get data on the attitudes, perceptions and behaviour of men and boys as well as young people related to various forms of violence; supporting advocacy, awareness-raising, community mobilization and educational programmes, as well as legal and policy reforms.

6
Findings and Conclusions

6.1 Summary of Findings

Violence against girls is a worldwide phenomenon that has devastating consequences in the lives of many. The state of Mizoram, where women and girls are believed to be respected is found to be no exception. Despite various awareness raising programmes and policies, girls in secondary schools often become victim of unwanted actions from their male students or teachers. Moreover, because of physical and sexual violence has been tolerated for so long, it has become a phenomenon that is resistant to change. This is reinforced by taboo, shame, and fear that resist speaking openly about it. Ironically, secondary schools have been found a place where different kinds of violence is tolerated and perpetrated by teachers as well as peer students. This research has aimed to give voice to boys, girls, parents and teachers, and by that get insight in their views on violence against girls in secondary schools of Mizoram.

Chapter 1 relating to introduction has been presented with a general outline of the issue at hand routed through its International, National and North East Indian Context. Theoretical aspects of girl-specific violence in school system have been highlighted next. The chapter terminates with a conceptual overview of types of gender-based violence on especially girl children in secondary schools.

An attempt is made in Chapter 2 to take stock of related literature so as to find the research gap and delineate the objectives of the study.

Review of Existing Literature was made under the headings such as studies on girl specific violence, nature of sexual violence, emotional and psychological violence, causes of such violence and rights/prevention of the child and global comparison of violence on women and girls. The objectives of the study are listed next as below:

1. To identify and classify the causes and the types of violence on girls in and around secondary schools of Mizoram;
2. To assess and establish the effects of violence on girls education in Mizoram;
3. To find out if there are policies and strategies dealing with violence against school girls and assess their effectiveness in tackling the problem;
4. To propose viable mechanisms and holistic ways of addressing the problem by stakeholders at all levels; and
5. To develop a framework for reduction of violence against girls in secondary schools of Mizoram.

Chapter 3 went on to discuss the research framework and methodology of the study. The research has followed the mixed mode method and has incorporated quantitative and qualitative methodologies to study the nature, nuances and the best practices adopted by the school for mitigating violence against girls in secondary schools. Multistage stratified random sampling procedures were adopted for the study. Accordingly, the sample comprised 4 Districts, 40 Secondary schools, 200 each from Students (Girls), Teachers and Parents, 8 personnel from NGOs and 4 Government Officials. The researcher has used both the Primary and Secondary data for this piece of research.

The fourth chapter presented the primary data collected from the field along with the analysis of the same under student's perceptions regarding the types of violent acts against girls in secondary schools, perceptions of teachers and parents, suggestion by teachers and parents and finally, effects of violence and abuse on girl's education. The results of this study support the view that violent act against girls in secondary schools is of concern to students, teachers, and parents in the state of Mizoram. Moreover, participants mentioned several kinds of aggressive and violent behaviours that occur often in their schools including fighting, beating, bullying, verbally and physically threatening others, and vandalism. Gang involvement, poor parental supervision, school staff victimization of students, and *en-route* intimidation due to location of school were perceived as contributing factors to school violence. Additionally, participants indicated that teachers also employed physical punishment such as, beating and insulting. In some cases, participants observed that school principals and colleagues tended to tolerate violence employed by teachers. It could be known that when victims and their parents could not cope with the situation they requested transfer to another school.

The respondents of this study emphasized the detrimental effects of violence against girls. Any physical, sexual or psychological assault perpetrated against school girls is likely to exasperate their already low profile of educational participation thereby making them less and less visible in the school or withdrawal by parents, denying girls their right to education and de-motivation towards class activities and home work. Victimized girls tend to leave their area and migrate to nearby towns and some of them end up being commercial sex workers. Sexual violence has damaging effects on the health of school girls such as exposing them to sexually transmitted diseases. The suggestions given by the participants have been consolidated at the end of the chapter.

Chapter five takes stock of the International, National and State specific policies, laws and instruments for the purpose of evaluating their implementation and to make a needs assessment in the context of Mizoram. It appears that there are glaring gaps in the infrastructure, set up and outreach services for students especially under secondary school system, as they exist now. Accordingly, a need based and time suited framework of policy for protection of crime against girl students studying in secondary schools is presented in this chapter so as to be able to tackle the problem of criminality and unjust practices in schools.

6.2 Conclusion

Looking back to the objectives and findings of the study, the conclusion of the study is presented hereunder:

Firstly, what stands out is the fact that the type of beatings that girls receive in the hands of their teachers in secondary school is not what one cold call severe or extreme. A majority of it was beating by a stick and a minor few got slapped or beaten by hand. A minor form of physical violence as punishment was also popular in the form of ear pulling. What is interesting here is that no one was caned or beaten with a belt. Aizawl and Champhai can be considered more urban and modern in terms of facilities and infrastructure; and these two districts reported very low cases of beating in the first place.

Facing sexual violence covered the issues of forced dating, kissing, sexual gestures, touching, attempts to rape, receiving of disturbing messages, and being forcefully shown unhealthy pictures. With regard to emotional and psychological violence, the girls in general did not feel rejection or neglect from teachers and fellow students. The teachers are said to request sex for marks or threaten repercussions if their sexual demands were not met.

In the case of verbal violence, although there was some amount of usage of bad words in the school premises, there were instances of ruthless degrading scolding. Some did feel that they were verbally being bullied by the teachers.

The cause of the different types of violence identified by the participants were "Poor supervision by school authorities", "Peer group influence", "Excessive use of mobile phones", "Lack of discipline in School", "Domestic conflict", "Violent behaviour exhibited by parents", "Adolescence period", "Imitation from mass media", "Lack of recreation", "Absence of teachers", "Lack of guidance and counselling", "Tuition given by teachers", "Partiality, prejudices, injustice by elder people", "Uncongenial school environment", and "Lack of interest in school".

The respondents were unanimous in feeling that girls, particularly in their adolescence, are more susceptible to aggressive behaviour and suffer more as a result. It has been conclusively found that the effects of violence on girls' education range from mental trauma, decreased self-esteem and confidence, dropping out of or withdrawal from schools, to evoking of even more non-conformist attitude without respect for the establishment and development of fear on the part of girls which tend to have more far fletching consequences.

Most of the policies in Mizoram are taken straight from Central schemes and are being tailor-made for the state, an evaluation revealed that there are much needed to be done. Specific policies in the context of violence against secondary school girls are yet unavailable either in Mizoram or in the country. Since the evidence shows that the inputs are not being translated into action, there is a need to realign focus system-wide on achieving violence free school and learning outcomes with due political commitments thereto.

The project posed a number of suggestions for Government, teachers and parents regarding dealing with issue of violence in schools. The suggestions include "Schools should organize awareness programmes on non-violence", "Mobile phones should be restricted for students in school campus", "Peace education programme must be included in school curriculum", "More time should be given to sports and other recreational activities on the curriculum", "Girls at risk of being violent must be helped individually", "Guidance and counselling units should be established to help students with behavioural problems", "Parents should visit the school of their children from time to time to know their wellbeing and progress", "Security arrangements should be made for school safety", "Girls should be taught self-defence through martial arts", and "Parent-teacher association should be made functional in every school" with Governmental support and funding irrespective of party in power. The policy framework suggested in this study go on to argue that the government's contribution is needed in the form of policies which may help prevention of violence on girls through Curriculum Restructuring, Co-curricular Activities, Whole School Approach, Teacher Training, Interdepartmental Coordination, Capacity building of Parents and Research.

Curriculum Restructuring and Co-curricular Activities may provide young people with tools and expertise to understand the root causes of violence in their communities, to educate and involve their peers and communities to prevent such violence, and to learn about where to access support if violence is experienced. Whole School Approach envisages that the entire school community must come together to agree on a strong and clear message that violence, sexual harassment, bullying and intolerance are unacceptable in the school environment. It is essential to ensure high quality teacher training (both scientific and pedagogical) in the implementation of the restructured curriculum. Teachers trained can be trainers elsewhere.

Elimination of violence against girls in schools requires interdepartmental co-ordination among all line departments, service providers and duty bearers. There is a need to identify roles and responsibilities of each line department and to inform them such as Police, Health, Education, W&CD Department of concerned state as the nodal department, District Administration, Law and Civil Society through policy notification. Similarly, the relationship between positive school climate and family involvement is reciprocal: each builds on the other. The involvement of parents in school needs to be strengthened for convergence of spheres of influence between home, school, and the community.

The Government is required to support in every branch of action suggested herein and to sponsor obtaining research data on the attitudes, perceptions and behaviour of men and boys as well as young people related to various forms of violence; supporting advocacy, awareness-raising, community mobilization and educational programmes, as well as legal and policy reforms. Finally, data collected from both primary and secondary sources go on to reveal the overarching study implications about types of violence, consequences, suggestions and policy framework. Thus, the outcome of the study is consolidated in the form in Table 6.1.

6.3 Recommendations

Based on the findings and conclusions of the study, the following recommendations have been put forward to all concerned institutions and stakeholders:

1. Train all teachers in non-violent methods of disciplining students. This subject should also be included in the education of teachers at teachers training colleges.
2. Include the peace education curriculum topics such as children's and women's rights (gender equality), effects of harmful traditional practices, effects of violence against/among girls and boys and on how to create harmonious and equal relationships between boys and girls.
3. The curriculum must also provide teachers with tools and methodologies for teaching students about these subjects.

Table 6.1: Types of Violence, Consequences, Suggestions and Policy Framework: The Study Outcome

Types of Violence	Examples	Consequences	Suggestions	Policy Framework
	Objective 1	**Objective 2**	**Objective 3**	**Objective 4**
Physical	Intention of causing physical pain, spanked, slapped, hit, shaken, pushed, kicked, beaten or belted	Lacerations and abrasions Brain injuries Bruises and welts Burns and scalds Fractures Ocular damage Abdominal/thoracic injuries, Irritable bowel syndrome	School Need to— 1. Develop a clear strategy that tackles violence against girls in Secondary schools. It is important to have a whole school approach that allows teachers, pupils, and administrative staff to work together on common goals for making schools safe. 2. Promote a more supportive culture by facilitating and enforcing the reporting of abuse, reducing bullying and corporal punishment, providing effective counselling, and encouraging constructive and equal relationships between students via positive role-modelling and explicit curricula and teaching/learning materials (i.e. life-skills-based sexuality education programmes with a gender and human rights perspective or peace education). 3. Become less authoritarian and more supportive to girls for personal development in coordination with PTA.	• Curriculum Restructuring, • Co-curricular Activities, • Whole School Approach • Teacher Training • Interdepartmental Coordination • Capacity building of Parents • Research.

(*Contd.*)

Types of Violence	Examples	Consequences	Suggestions	Policy Framework
Sexual	Fondling a child's genitals, making the child fondle the adult's genitals, intercourse, rape, sodomy, exhibitionism and sexual exploitationmaking the child exhibit private body parts, exhibiting private body parts to a child, photographing a child in the nude, Sexual advances, forcible kissing, forced to view pornographic materials, Gender discrimination.	Sexual dysfunction Reproductive health problems. Sexually transmitted diseases, including HIV/AIDS. Unwanted pregnancy.	4. Foster collaboration with relevant NGOs especially ICPS and DCPUs working on violence against girls, rape, sexual assault, child abuse, HIV/AIDS and sexuality education for the purposes of providing training, counselling, and advocacy services within the schools. 5. Consider engaging peer educators (adolescents or young adults who can visit schools to talk to pupils about sexual violence and other issues that concern them), as is currently being done. 6. Ensure that safe and secure toilet facilities are available for girls. 7. Schools must arrange appropriate surveillance system for safe and smooth journey of girls to and from school. 8. The prompt and effective investigation of such complaints; prompt and appropriate disciplinary action including due process protections for the persons alleged to have perpetrated the offense. **Community** 1. Create an enabling consensus environment so that local schools, communities, and NGOs can adapt both formal and non-formal education models to make the commute to and from school safe and secure for children.	

(*Contd.*)

Types of Violence	Examples	Consequences	Suggestions	Policy Framework
Psychological	Verbal abuse, mental abuse, and emotional maltreatment, threatening or terrorizing, belittling or rejecting treatment, using derogatory terms to describe the child, habitual tendency to blame the child or make her a scapegoat.	Stress, Fear and Stigma. Cognitive impairment. Retaliatory and risk-taking behaviours. Depression and anxiety. Developmental delays. Eating and sleep disorders. Feelings of shame and guil. Hyperactivity. Poor relationships. Poor school performance. Poor self-esteem. Post-traumatic stress disorder. Psychosomatic disorders. Suicidal behaviour and self-harm.	2. Raise community awareness and promote community support for educating girls and work closely with schools, ministries, and NGOs to tackle violence in the home, within communities, and in schools. School NSS programme need to be welcome in the communities for mobilisation and awareness generation. 3. Self-defence Centre for Girl Child will be established in partnership with All Mizoram Karate Association (AMKA) and Mizoram Amateur Taekwondo Association (MATA). **Family** 1. Parents should inquire from their children what problems they are facing and find ways to solve the problems. 2. Parents should provide the good and effective environment in the home. The atmosphere of Love in family will help cure a violent attitude towards others. 3. The parents should make their influence felt in the kind of friends that their children relate with daily.	

(Contd.)

Types of Violence	Examples	Consequences	Suggestions	Policy Framework
			4. Parents need to take time out for parental counselling at school and to take PTA engagement as their priority. 5. PTA to facilitate interpersonal communication and shared parenting practices 6. Parents can take help of counsellors and psychiatrists in order to provide guidance in career, academics, social and personal issues. 7. Parents keep an eye on their wards about not to regular watching of violent serials, movies or playing aggressive games in mobiles and parents should check the message box and what's app and face book of their children. 8. Parents should go regularly to meet teachers in order to understand the current position of their child. 9. Parents should not compare their children with the success and failure of other children. 10. Parents are advised that they should behave like friends with their children for understanding the problems.	

(*Contd.*)

Types of Violence	Examples	Consequences	Suggestions	Policy Framework
			Government 1. Adopt a national plan of action for reducing violence against girls in secondary school. 2. Develop in-service training programmes for experienced teachers on the prevention of, and response to, violence against girls. 3. Offer these workshops throughout the country. Appoint a faculty member within each teacher training college to coordinate training and research efforts. 4. Help teachers explore their own attitudes and personal experiences regarding gender-based violence, sexuality, and HIV/AIDS so they can be more effective in working with their students and colleagues. 5. Educate teachers on their responsibilities under any code of conduct that is developed. 6. Establish the new Special and Observation Homes sanctioned by the Ministry of Women and Child Development in the districts not having such homes. 7. Separate the Observation Homes and Special Homes at Aizawl and Lunglei. 8. Implement SABALA Programme in all the districts of Mizoram.	

4. Strengthen gender curriculum that includes family planning and age based sex education at Teacher Training Colleges and schools and continuously educate and create awareness among school communities to stop physical and emotional abuses through provision of training to teachers and school guards, unit leaders, classroom monitors, record keepers, and other school community members.
5. Responsible government bodies must apply a system for follow up, reporting and ensuring action is taken to enforce the implementation of school rules and regulations. For instance, educational institutions at various levels must constantly monitor report and take action against malpractices such as corporal punishment in schools. Advocate for revision of the existing school rules and regulations and their effective implementation.
6. Establish and strengthen child rights clubs for children in secondary schools.
7. Establish and strengthen girls' clubs and boys clubs for girls and boys respectively in secondary schools. The clubs shall be empowered to give peer education, report and follow up on violence and abuse in and around the school.
8. Strengthen the HIV/AIDS clubs and ensure the clubs include topics such as family planning, use of condoms and effects of sexual and gender based violence.
9. Raise the awareness among parents and communities about the rights of children in general and rules and regulations by the Ministry of Education as well as local school rules and regulations in particular.
10. Strengthen the communication between school and parents, through the PTAs. The school authorities shall be proactive and reach out to the parents in the communities.
11. Make sure schools have separated toilets for girls and that the toilets are not placed in a remote part of the school compound.
12. Establish a mechanism at school level to support girls in reporting violence and abuse and to provide appropriate counselling and other necessary support victims of violence.
13. Increase awareness about the negative effect of harmful

traditional practices within the local communities. General awareness campaigns must be supported by concrete mobilization of religious and community leaders, including health professionals, educators,

14. Involve NGOs and YMA in community mobilization and creation of girls protection structures (including the way to and from school) and in general awareness raising and mobilization for the promotion of human and child rights.
15. Work closely with DEOs and BEOs to change the attitude of parents to a culture, which promotes open dialogues with children on child rights, values and benefits of girls' education.

Others (National Level/Concerned Government Bodies)

1. Develop into concrete strategies for actual implementation of polices of relevance to protection of girls and boys against any type of violence, for instance Developmental Social Welfare Policy and Strategy.
2. Strengthen and support the national framework for monitoring of the CRC implementation at all levels.
3. Improve the attitude and capacity of the law enforcement authorities when it comes to violence against secondary school girls.
4. Punishment against the perpetrators should be more severe and the legal process has to be short and effective. Perpetrators should get the legal punishment they deserve.
5. Reduce the range of punishments imposed on offenders of violence and abuse against secondary school girls..
6. Undertake advocacy work concerning violence and abuse against children in general and school girls in particular through public mobilization and participation by in the school system, local state structures, the media, and government.

Ministry of Women and Child Development

Ministry of Women and Child Development can:

1. Adopt a national plan of action for gender-based violence in schools.

2. Provide guidelines to schools detailing the appropriate response to allegations by students of rape, sexual assault, or harassment, whether by teachers or fellow students, including sections relating to: (a) the creation of accessible school procedures by which students can make confidential complaints; (b) the prompt and effective investigation of such complaints; (c) prompt and appropriate disciplinary action including due process protections for the persons alleged to have perpetrated the offense; (d) referral to the criminal justice system; and e) support services;
3. Develop a code of conduct for teachers and students that expressly prohibit gender violence in schools. The code of conduct should be distributed to all schools and its contents widely publicized among those in the education system. Teachers should be obliged to follow the code of conduct as part of their employment contract;
4. Implement and support comprehensive sexuality/sexual health education in schools, placing violence against women as an integral part of the content;
5. Collaborate with other ministries and civil society (including the private sector) in national campaigns on the radio and TV, and in print media on the negative effects, including how to prevent it and where teachers, students, and parents can turn for help; and
6. Create an enabling policy environment so that local schools, communities, and NGOs can adapt both formal and non-formal education models to make the commute to and from school safe and secure for girls.

6.4 Implication for Further Research

1. The problems found during the project shows the uniqueness of the position of women in Mizo society. While on one hand, Mizos follow patriarchal norms, on the other, the women experience relatively high level of freedom. This information is evident in the data gathered for the project and can be used as a foundation for feminist studies based case studies of the Mizo society.

2. Considering the difference in the data taken from more urban locations of Aizawl and Champhai as opposed to Kolasib and Mamit, one can use the project's findings as a foundation to research on the topics of impact of modernisation and urbanisation on education in Mizoram.
3. In general research studies on violence, one can use the project as a foundation to try and find out why Mizoram has such low levels of violence and crime.
4. The focus of this study was mainly on secondary school girls. As a result of this, the prevalence and extent of violence against girls in primary schools and higher education institutions were not adequately treated. Therefore, there is a need for undertaking further study on the problems of these groups of girls.
5. The focus of this study was mainly on violence against school girls. However, the problem of violence is not limited to this group. This calls for further study to address problems related to violence against non-school and out of school girls.
6. It is believed that integrating the results of this study with other studies will enable concerned bodies to develop a comprehensive strategy and policy on violence and abuse confronting the girl child.

Appendix-A
Interview Schedule for Teachers and Parents

Respected Sir/Madam,

These questionnaires consist of statements about the causes of violence against girls in secondary schools. The questions pertain to your opinion towards the causes of violence against girls in secondary school along with some suggestions to reduce the same. I assure you that the information you give will be kept highly confidential and will not be divulged to anybody. It will be used purely for research purpose only. There are three possible answers to each question. You should answer each question either as 'YES' or 'NO' by putting tick (✓) marks in the appropriate brackets. Mark the last answer, i.e. 'UNDECIDED' only when it is impossible to say 'Yes' or 'No'.

Thanking you.

PERSONAL INFORMATION

Age :____________________

Sex :____________________

Religion :____________________

Qualification :____________________

Experience :____________________

Sl. No.	Statements	Yes	No	Undecided
1.	Poor supervision by school authorities often leads to violence in schools	( )	( )	( )
2.	Peer group influence is the common	( )	( )	( )

cause of violence among students

3. The reason of violent behaviour is lack of interest in School ( ) ( ) ( )
4. The reason of violence among students is lack of discipline in the school ( ) ( ) ( )
5. Domestic conflict is responsible for violence among students ( ) ( ) ( )
6. Violent behaviour exhibit by parents has a great influence on children ( ) ( ) ( )
7. Violence exists against girls in secondary schools because students go through their adolescence period ( ) ( ) ( )
8. Imitation of the improper and violent behaviour through mass media causes violence ( ) ( ) ( )
9. Lack of recreational opportunities and facilities is the common cause of violence ( ) ( ) ( )
10. Students exhibit violent action due to their emotional instability ( ) ( ) ( )
11. Violence is more likely to happen when there is too many free periods ( ) ( ) ( )
12. Absence of teachers from classrooms makes students restless which in turn cause violence ( ) ( ) ( )
13. Violence among students is due to partiality, prejudices and injustice done to the child by the parents, elders and teachers. ( ) ( ) ( )
14. Violence used to occur because there is lack of guidance and counselling ( ) ( ) ( )
15. Tuition practices by teachers can lead to different types of violence ( ) ( ) ( )
16. Uniform Discipline Policies do not meet the different needs of the students which in turn cause violence ( ) ( ) ( )
17. The common cause of violence is use of Mobile Phones by the students ( ) ( ) ( )

18. Aggressive nature is the cause of violent actions ( ) ( ) ( )
19. Attracting to opposite sex leads to sexual violence ( ) ( ) ( )
20. Violence occur more in uncongenial school environment ( ) ( ) ( )
21. Parents should provide basic needs for their children ( ) ( ) ( )
22. More time should be given to sports and other recreational activities on the curriculum ( ) ( ) ( )
23. Girls at risk of being violent must be helped individually ( ) ( ) ( )
24. Games, debate, excursions and club activities should be encouraged ( ) ( ) ( )
25. More activities should be included in the teaching programmes ( ) ( ) ( )
26. Guidance and counselling units should be established to help students with behavioural problems ( ) ( ) ( )
27. Parents should visit the school of their children from time to time to know their behaviour ( ) ( ) ( )
28. The school environment should be improved to reduce violence ( ) ( ) ( )
29. Security arrangements should be made for school safety ( ) ( ) ( )
30. School staffs should be trained occasionally ( ) ( ) ( )
31. Peace club should be established in each school ( ) ( ) ( )
32. Grievance and redressal cell should be opened in every school ( ) ( ) ( )
33. Peace education programme must be included in school curriculum ( ) ( ) ( )
34. Mobile phones should be restricted for students in school campus ( ) ( ) ( )

35. School should organize awareness programmes on non-violence ( ) ( ) ( )
36. There must be professional counselor in each school ( ) ( ) ( )
37. Parents Teachers Association should be established in every school ( ) ( ) ( )

Apendix-B
Interview Schdule for Students

Dear Participant,

Please express your opinion! The purpose of this study is to measure the meaning of certain concepts related to violence against girls in secondary schools. Some questions are given below and they are concerned with your experiences. There are three possible answers to each question. You should answer each question either as 'YES' or 'NO' by putting tick (✓) marks in the appropriate brackets. Mark the last answer, i.e. 'UNDECIDED' only when it is impossible to say 'Yes' or 'No'. You have to read each question carefully and put your answers in the proper place. Please answer all the questions without any fear and hesitation as your responses will be kept confidential.

Sl. No.	Statements	Yes	No	Undecided
1.	Did any of your teachers beat you? If yes, please specify.			
	(a) Cane	( )	( )	( )
	(b) Duster	( )	( )	( )
	(c) Stick	( )	( )	( )
	(d) Belt	( )	( )	( )
2.	Did any of your teachers beat any of the girls?			
	(a) Cane	( )	( )	( )
	(b) Duster	( )	( )	( )
	(c) Stick	( )	( )	( )
	(d) Belt	( )	( )	( )

3. Did any of your teachers slap you?	( )	( )	( )
4. Have you experienced fighting with your schoolmates in the school premises?	( )	( )	( )
5. Did any of the students steal your belongings?	( )	( )	( )
6. Did your teacher punish you by pinching your ear?	( )	( )	( )
7. Have you experienced other students seizing your food?	( )	( )	( )
8. Did any of your schoolmates intentionally step on you or push you?	( )	( )	( )
9. Have you ever feel lonely, or ignored among your peers?	( )	( )	( )
10. Have you ever feel neglected by your teachers?	( )	( )	( )
11. Have you ever feel rejected among your peers?	( )	( )	( )
12. Have your teachers not acknowledged or rejected you?	( )	( )	( )
13. Do you ever get humiliated or get scolded unruly by your teachers in front of others?	( )	( )	( )
14. Did any of the teachers ever touch restricted part of your body?	( )	( )	( )
15. Did any of your schoolmates ever touch restricted part of your body by force?	( )	( )	( )
16. Did any boys from your school ever try to have sex with you by threatening you?	( )	( )	( )
17. Did any teacher ever try to have sex with you?	( )	( )	( )
18. Have any of your teachers ever showed you any type of unhealthy pictures?	( )	( )	( )
19. Have any of the boys from your school tried to kiss you by force?	( )	( )	( )

20. Have any of your teachers tried to kiss you by force? ( ) ( ) ( )
21. Have you ever received any kind of message or letters relating to sexual abuse? ( ) ( ) ( )
22. Did any of your teachers ever bully you or your friend orally with sexual words? ( ) ( ) ( )
23. Had any of the students tried to molest you or any of your friends? ( ) ( ) ( )
24. Has any teacher from your school tried to molest you or any of your friend? ( ) ( ) ( )
25. Do teachers humiliate you in front of your classmates when you give wrong answer(s)? ( ) ( ) ( )
26. Did your teacher reject your request to leave the class or school when you have your menstruation period? ( ) ( ) ( )
27. Did any of your teachers tease you when seeking permission to leave the class or school for reasons to do with menstruation? ( ) ( ) ( )
28. Did any of your teachers made sexual gestures to you or to any other girl? ( ) ( ) ( )
29. Did any of the male students made sexual gestures to you? ( ) ( ) ( )
30. Did you experience any of the teachers used bad or abusive language against you? ( ) ( ) ( )
31. Did any of your schoolmates try to assault you by making persistent remarks on physical appearance and body size? ( ) ( ) ( )
32. Did any of your teachers try to assault you by making persistent remarks on physical appearance and body size? ( ) ( ) ( )
33. Did any of your teachers asked you for a date? ( ) ( ) ( )

34. Did any of the boys from your school try to take you on a date forcefully?	( )	( )	( )
35. Did any of your teachers touch your breast without your consent?	( )	( )	( )
36. Did any of your schoolmates touch your breast without your consent?	( )	( )	( )
37. Did any of your teachers threaten you to punish for refusing sex?	( )	( )	( )
38. Had any of your teachers insulted you with sexual language?	( )	( )	( )
39. Had any of the students from your school insulted you with sexual language?	( )	( )	( )
40. Did any of your teachers ask you to have sex for marks?	( )	( )	( )
41. Have you ever experienced an attempt of rape?	( )	( )	( )

Appendix-C
FGD Questions

Teachers and Parents

1. Do you think that violence against girls will affect the enrolment ratio?
2. Do the school provide good facilities like separate toilets to the girls?
3. Have you allotted any female teacher for taking care of violence against girls?
4. Do you feel a separate cell will be open for addressing violence against girls?
5. What measures have you taken for mitigating violence against girls?
6. Do you feel girls are not attentive in classrooms?
7. Is there any effect of violence in girl's education?
8. Are there any effects of Violence on Girls' to Complete Homework?
9. Are there any effects of Violence on School Girls' Future Life?

Girl Students

1. Are you facing any violence in the school premises?
2. What type of violence are you facing in the campus?
3. Do you think that it will affect your education?
4. Do your parents deny attending school?
5. Are any teacher allotted for taking care of your hygienic needs?

6. Is there any separate toilet for you?
7. Do you need a separate special cell to address your problems?

Government Officials and NGO Personnel

1. How many cases on violence against girls you find in secondary schools of Mizoram?
2. What are the plans and programmes implemented by the government of Mizoram for eradicating violence against girls in secondary schools?
3. Is there any awareness programme you have organized in secondary schools relating to this?
4. What are the activities taken by NGOs for removing the violence against girls in secondary schools?

Appendix-D
Photographs

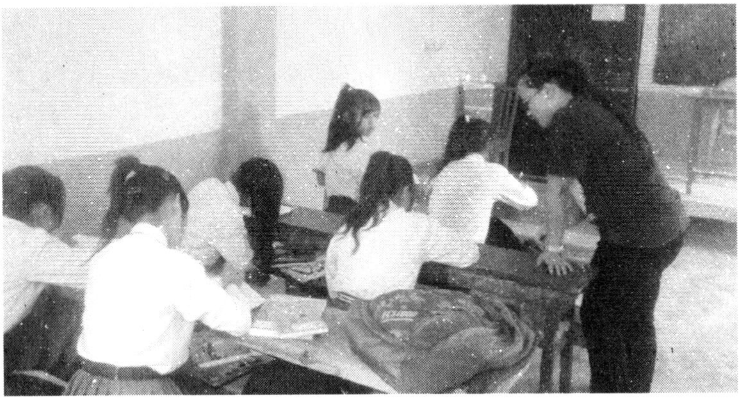

Data collection from Champhai district

Collection of data from the high school students

Data collection from Kolasib High School

Interviewing a Secondary School Teachers

Interviewing the Secondary School Girls

Interview with Government officials

FGD with Government officials

Interview with Government officials

Bibliography

Abuya, B.A., Onsomu, E.O. and Moore, D. (2012). "Educational Challenges and Diminishing Family Safety Net Faced by High-School Girls in a Slum Residence, Nairobi, Kenya". *International Journal of Educational Development*, 32: 81-91.

Abuya, B.A., Onsomu, E.O., Moore, D. and Piper, C.N. (2012). "Association Between Education and Domestic Violence among Women Being Offered an HIV Test in Urban and Rural Areas in Kenya". *Journal of Interpersonal Violence*, 27: 2022-2038.

ACHR (2013). *State of Juvenile Justice in Mizoram*, Asian Centre for Human Rights, Janakpuri, New Delhi.

Action Aid International (2004). *Stop Violence against Girls in School: research briefing*, Johannesburg: Action Aid International.

Action Aid International (2012). *A Theory of Change for Tackling Violence Against Women and Girls*, London: Action Aid International.

Alam, N., Roy, S.K., Ahmed, T. (2010). "Sexually Harassing Behaviour against Adolescent Girls in Rural Bangladesh: implications for achieving millennium development goals". *Journal of Interpersonal Violence*, Vol 25, Issue 3, pp. 443-456.

Andria, B. Eisman, Sarah, A. Stoddard, Justin Heinze, Cleopatra H. Caldwell, and Marc A. Zimmerman (2015). *Depressive Symptoms, Social Support and Violence Exposure Among Urban Youth: A Longitudinal Study of Resilience* Sep, 51(9): 1307-1316. Published online doi: 10.1037/a0039501

Asmara Figue, Akanksha Marphatia, Victorine Djitrinou, Jenny Parkes (2010). Girls at the Heart: a review of girls' participation in initiatives to combat violence in school, paper presented at E4 conference: Engendering Empowerment: Education and Equality, Dakar, Senegal.

Astor, R.A., Meyer, H.A., & Behre, W. J. (1999). "Unwanted Places and Times: Maps and Interviews about Violence in High Schools". *American Educational Research Journal*, 36, 3-42.

Benbenishty, R., Astor, A.R. (2005). *School Violence Embedded in Context.* Oxford, UK: Oxford University Press.

Bhatnagar, A. (1997). Guidance and counselling. In: Buch, M.B. (Ed.), *Fifth survey of educational research 1988-1992*, (Vol 1, pp. 216-234). New Delhi: National Council of Educational Research and Training.

Bhana, Deevia (2012). "Girls are not free", In and out of the South African school. *International Journal of Educational Development* 32(2).

Birnbaum, A., Lytle, L.A., Murray, D.M., Story, M., Perry, C.L., Boutelle, K.N., (2002). "Survey Development to Assess Correlates of Young Adolescents' Eating". *American Journal of Health Behaviour*, 26(4), 284-295.

Boyer, Wanda (2008). "Girl-to-Girl Violence: The Voice of the Victims". Childhood Education Research Library, *ProQuest*. 84.6 344-350.

Camacho, K., Ehrensaft, M.K., Cohen, P. (2012). "Exposure to Intimate Partner Violence, Peer Relations, and Risk for Internalizing Behaviours: A Prospective Longitudinal Study". *Jan* 27(1):125-41.

Catherine Rothon, Jenny Head, Emily Klineberg, and Stephen Stansfelda (2011). Can social support protect bullied adolescents from adverse outcomes? A prospective study on the effects of bullying on the educational achievement and mental health of adolescents at secondary schools in East London. Jun; 34(3): 579-588.doi: 10.1016/j.adolescence.2010.02.007

Chen, J.K., & Astor, R.A. (2009a). "The Perpetration of School Violence in Taiwan: An Analysis of Gender, Grade Level, and School Type". *School Psychology International*, 30, 568-584.

Chen, J.K., & Astor, R.A. (2009b). "Students' Reports of Violence against Teachers in Taiwanese Schools". *Journal of School Violence*, 8(1), 2-17.

Chen, J.K., & Astor, R.A. (in press). "School Violence Perpetration in Taiwan: Examining How Western Risk Factors Predict School Violence in an Asian Culture". *Journal of Interpersonal Violence.*

Chen, X. (2000). "Growing Up in a Collectivistic Culture: Socialization and Socio-emotional Development in Chinese Children". *Human development in cross-cultural perspective* (pp. 331-353), Lengerich, Germany.

David, B. Mykota, Adele Laye (2015). Violence Exposure and Victimization among Rural Adolescents, *Canadian Journal of School Psychology.*

Deb, S. (2006). *Children in Agony: A Sourcebook.* New Delhi: Concept Publishing Company.

Deb, S., Mukherjee, A. (2009). *Impact of Sexual Abuse on Mental Health of Children.* New Delhi: Concept Publishing Company.

Education for Change Ltd. (2013), Final Evaluation Report to Stop Violence against Girls in School.

Finkelhor, David (2007). "The Comprehensive Study of Childhood Victimizations". In, Davis, R.C., Luirigio, A.J., & Herman, S. (Eds.), *Victims of crime* (3rd ed) (pp. 9-34). Thousand Oaks, CA: Sage Publications.

Gådin, K.G. (2012). Sexual harassment of girls in elementary school: a concealed phenomenon within a heterosexual romantic discourse. *J Interferes Violence.* Jun; 27(9):1762-79. doi: 10.1177/0886260511430387.

Gagné, M.H. (2001). *Les parties parental psychological equipment violence's: A Threat to Children's Mental Health.* 20, 75-106.

Gagné, M.H., Lavoie, F., Fortin, A. (2003). *Development of the Psychologically Violent Parental Practices Inventory*, 35, 268-280.

Ghosh, Ratna, Chakravarti, Paromita, Mansi Kumari (2015). *Women's Empowerment and Education: Panchayats and Women's Self-Help Groups in India.*

Gillander Gådin, K., Ahlgren, C., Weiner, G. (2011). "School Health Promotion to Increase Empowerment, Gender Equality and Pupil

Participation: A Focus Group Study of a Swedish Elementary School Initiative". *Scandinavian Journal of Educational Research.*

GOI and Save The Children, Prayas (2007). "Study on Child Abuse in India." Government of India. Ministry of Women & Child Development, *Report*, 71-103.

GOI (2007). *Study on Child Abuse.* India, Ministry of Women and Child Development, Government of India.

Gracia, E. (2004). "Unreported cases of domestic violence against women: towards an epidemiology of social silence, tolerance, and inhibition". *J Epidermal Community Health*, 58: 536-7. [PMC free article] [PubMed]

Consequences of Domestic Violence on Women's Mental Health in Bosnia and Herzegovina.

Gorman-Smith, D., Tolan, G.F., Zelli, A., Huesmann, L.R. (1996). "The Relation of Family Functioning to Violence among Inner-City Minority Youth", *Journal of Family Psychology*, 38: 4: 538-550.

Greene, M., Robles, O., Stout, K. and Suvilaakso, T. (2013). *A girl's right to learn without fear: Working to end gender-based violence at school.* Woking: Plan International.

Hamelin, C., Salomon, C., Cyr D., Gueguen, A., Lert, F. (2010). *Childhood Sexual Abuse and Adult Sexual Health among Indigenous Kanak Women and Non-Kanak Women of New Caledonia.* Sep 34(9): 677-88.

Heather, A., Sears, E. Sandra Byers, E. Lisa Price (2007). "The Co-occurrence of Adolescent Boys' and Girls' Use of Psychologically, Physically, and Sexually Abusive Behaviours in Their Dating Relationships".*Journal of Adolescence.* Volume 30, Issue 3, pp. 487-504.

Hyder and Malik (2007). "Violence against Children: A Challenge for Public Health in Pakistan", *Journal of Health Ppul Nutrition*, 25(2); ttps://www.ncbi.nlm.nih.gov/pmc/articles/PMC2753994/

Ji-Kang Chen, Hsi-Sheng Wei (2011). *The Impact of School Violence on Self-Esteem and Depression Among Taiwanese Junior High School Students.* DOI: 10.1007/s11205-010-9625-4

Johnston, L.D., O'Malley, P.M., & Bachman, J.G. (1996). "National Survey Results on Drug Use from the Monitoring the Future Study,

1975-1995.Vol. 1, Secondary School Students (NIH Publication No. 96-4139)".

Karagün, Elif (2015). "Violence Tendencies of High School Students: An Examination in Terms of Exposure to Violence, Participation in Sports and Socio-demographic Attributes. *Educational Research and Reviews*, Vol. 10, No. 1, pp. 29-35.

Khoury-Kassabri, M. (2006). "Student Victimization by Educational Staff in Israel". *Child Abuse & Neglect*, 30, 691-707.

Khoury-Kassabri, M., Benbenishty, R., Astor, R., Zeira, A. (2004). "The Contribution of Community, Family and School Variables on Student Victimization". *American Journal of Community Psychology*, 34,187-204.

Krug, E.G. *et al.*, (eds.) (2002). *World Report on Violence and Health.* Geneva, World Health Organization,

Kury, Helmut *et al.* (eds.) (2016). *Women and Children as Victims and Offenders: Background, Prevention, Reintegration*, Springer International Publishing, Switzerland.

Lavoie, F., Pacaud, M.C., Roy, M., Lebossé, C. (2007). "An Awareness and Prevention Programme for Teens (16-17 Years Old) Focusing on Abuse in Dating Relationships and Sexual Harassment".

Leach, M., Slade, E. and Dunne, M. (2012). *Promising Practice in School-Related Gender Based Violence (SRGBV) Prevention and Response Programming Globally*, Brighton: University of Sussex.

Lytle, L.A., & Perry, C.L. (2001). "Applying Research and Theory in Programme Planning: An Example from a Nutrition Education Intervention". *Health Promotion Planning*, 2(1), 68-80.

Melançon, C., Gagné, M.H. (2011). "Father's and Mother's Psychological Violence and Adolescent Behavioural Adjustment". *Journal of Interpersonal Violence*, 26, 991-1011.

Michelle, M. (2011). Domestic violence against women with learning disabilities. Paper presents independent research commissioned/ funded by the NIHR School for Social Care Research.

Michael, J. Mann, Alfgeir, L. Kristjansson, Inga Dora Sigfusdottir, Megan, L. (2015). *The Role of Community, Family, Peer, and School Factors in Group Bullying: Implications for School-Based Intervention.* Volume 85, Issue 7, pp. 413-496.

Miller-Johnson, S., Coie, J.D., Maumary-Gremaud, A., Bierman K. (2002). Conduct Problems Prevention Research Group. Peer rejection and aggression and early starter models of conduct disorder. *Journal of Abnormal Child Psychology*, 30: 217-230.

Mohanty, R.K. (2015a). "Private and Public Dichotomy about Domestic Violence: The State of the Art Literature on Issues and Concerns" in Asha Shukla (ed.), *Crime against Women*, Serials Publishing, New Delhi, pp. 227-268.

Mohanty, R.K. (2016b). "Crime against Girl Child: Victimology of Vulnerabilities and Victimizations", *Contemporary Social Scientist*, Volume 8, Number 1.

Mohanty, R.K. (2016c). "The Predicament of Girl Child in India: The State of the Art Literature on Issues and Concerns", Mizoram University, *Journal of Humanities and Social Sciences*, Volume 2, Number 2, pp. 140-160.

Mohanty, R.K. (2016d). "Sociology of Recidivism in North East India: Exploring the Scope for Further Research", *Contemporary Social Scientist*, Volume 8, Number 2, pp. 64-83.

Mona Khoury-Kassabri,Tahany Gadalla, Joanne Daciuk (2005). "Risk factors for involvement in cyber bullying: Victims, bullies and bully-victims", *Children and Youth Services Review,* 34 (2012) 63-70.

Monica H. Swahn, Thomas R. Simon, Ileana Arias, Robert M. Bossarte (2008). "Measuring Sex Differences in Violence, Victimization and Perpetration Within Date and Same-Sex Peer Relationships". *Journal of Interpersonal Violence*. Vol. 23, Issue 8, pp. 1120-1138.

Murray, D.M., & Short, B.J. (1996). "Infraclass Correlation among Measures Related to Alcohol Use by School Aged Adolescents: Estimates, Correlates, and Applications in Intervention Studies". *Journal of Drug Education*, 26(3), 207-230.

Nikki van der Gaag (2011). "'Because I am a Girl' Group Finds Boys Matter, too". PLAN International, *Toronto Star*.

Orpinas, P., Horne, A.M. (2004). "Multisite Violence Prevention Project. A Teacher-Focused Approach to Prevent and Reduce Students' Aggressive Behaviour": The GREAT Teacher Programme, *American Journal of Preventive Medicine*, 26: 29-38.

Orpinas, P., Nahapetyan, L., Song, X., McNicholas, C., & Reeves, P.M. (2012b). "Psychological Dating Violence Perpetration and Victimization: Trajectories from Middle to High School". *Aggressive Behaviour*, 38(6), 510-520.

Osler, A. and Hill, J. (1999). "Exclusion from School and Racial Equality: An Examination of Government Proposals in the Light of Recent Research Evidence". *Cambridge Journal of Education*, 29(1): 33-62.

Parkes, J. and Heslop, J. (2011). *Stop Violence against Girls in School: A cross-country analysis of baseline research from Ghana, Kenya and Mozambique*, London: Action Aid International.

Rege, Sharmila (2004). *Sociology of Gender*, OUP. New Delhi.

Save the Children Sweden (2010). Regional Study of Children's Participation in Southern Africa: South Africa, Swaziland and Zambia, Save the Children Sweden.

Save the Children, Denmark; Ministry of Education & Ministry of Women Affairs (2008). "A Study on Violence against Girls in Primary Schools and its Impacts on Girl's Education in Ethiopia". Retrieved from http://www.ungei.org/resources/files/study_on_violence_Against_schoolgfils_final_pdf

Schuler, M. (ed.) (1992). *Freedom from Violence: Women's Strategies from Around the World.* New York: UNIFEM.

Sen, Amartya (2001). Many Facets of Gender Inequality, *The Frontline*, 18 (22), Oct 27-Nov. 09.

Sen, Amartya (2006). *Identity and Violence: The Illusion of Destiny*, W.W. Norton & Company.

Sibnath Deb, Kerryann,W. (2012). "Impact of physical, psychological, and sexual violence on social adjustment of school children in India", *School Psychology International*, Vol 33, Issue 4.

Shen, A.C.T. (2008). "Coping Strategies of Dating Violence: A National Study of Taiwanese College Students". Paper presented at the International Family Aggression Society Conference, Preston, UK.

Shen, A.C., Chiu, M.Y.L., Gao, J. (2012). Predictors of dating violence among Chinese adolescents: The role of gender-role beliefs and justification of violence. *Journal of Interpersonal Violence.* 2012; 27(6):1066-1089. doi: 10.1177/0886260511424497

Sinha, Shantha (2008). *Protection of Girls and Their Rights, Keynote address at the Symposium on "Girl Child"*, Panjab University, Chandigarh.

Sullivan, T.N., Farrell, A.D., Kliewer W. Peer (2006). "Victimization in Early Adolescence: Association Between Physical and Relational Victimization and Drug Use, Aggression, and Delinquent Behaviours among Urban Middle School Students". *Development and Psychopathology*, 18: 119-137.

Susana, T. (2003). *Violence against women.* The President and Fellows of Harvard College are collaborating with JSTOR to digitize, preserve, and extend access to Health and Human Rights www.jstor.org https://cdn2.sph.harvard.edu/wp-content/uploads/sites/13/2014/04/6-Fried.pdf

Terry, Geraldine and J. Hoare (2007). *Gender-based Violence*, Oxfam GB, London.

Tora, A. (2013). *Assessment of sexual violence against female students in Wolaita Sodo.* Jul; 28(11):2351-67. doi: 10.1177/0886260512475316.

United Nations General Assembly Declaration (1993) on the Elimination of Violence against Women.

UNESCO & UNICEF (2013). Making Education a Priority in the Post-2015 Development Agenda: Report of the global thematic consultation on education in the post-2015 development agenda, UNESCO, UNICEF.

UNRIC (2013). "Key Statistics on Violence Against Women and Girls", online at: http://www.unric.org/en/uk-a-ireland-news-archive/28258-key-statistics-on-violence-against-women-and-girls-

Vacha Kishori Project Team (2011). Pre-adolescent Girls in Municipal Schools in Mumbai, *Economic and Political Weekly*, Vol. 37, Issue No. 17.

Visaria, L. (2000). Violence against women in India: Evidence from Rural Gujarat. Gujarat Institute of Development Studies. In *Domestic Violence in India, A Summary Report of Three Studies.* International Center for Research on Women, Washington, DC, September, 14-25.

Violence & Victimization Research Division's Compendium of Research On Violence Against Women 1993-2005, 1998-WT-VX-0014, p. 35, 1999-WT-VX-0014, p. 59.

Wei, H.S., & Chen, J.K. (2009). "Social Withdrawal, Peer Rejection and Victimization: An Examination of Path Models", *Journal of School Violence,* 8(1), 18-28.

WHO (2013). *Adolescent Pregnancy,* online at: http://www.who.int/maternal_child_adolescent/topics/maternal/adolescent_pregnancy/en/

Yankah, E. (2011). Mid-Term Review of Stop Violence against Girls in School Project, unpublished mid-term project evaluation report.

Index